The
Digital Firm

. . . .

How to change your accounting firm to remain competitive

FARNELL

www.willfarnell.com
www.farnellclarke.co.uk
www.linkedin.com/willfarnell

Contents

Foreword

· ·

I've known Will for many years and worked closely with him – not only as a software partner, but also during my research of the accountant's role for an internal IRIS project.

I've always viewed Will's firm as a technology pathfinder, putting them a few years ahead of the majority of accountants. Through the trial, testing and implementation of various technologies (good and bad), Will has gained valuable insight into what works for a digital firm. He has hit a few bumps along the way and found a few pitfalls, but that only adds to the experience and helps fine-tune processes to ultimately improve efficiency and customer experience.

At a time when using and embracing the latest technology is a vital part of doing business, the majority of accountants know they need to change and, in some cases, want to evolve. But while the right tools are available, they lack the knowledge and experience to take the first step and cross the digital divide. As HMRC's MTD becomes a reality in the next 12 months, accounting practices need help to fully embrace the opportunity it represents.

For me, this is where Will is unique – not only has he worked out and fine-tuned what works well from a technology and process point of view, but more importantly he wants to share his valuable experience with the rest of the UK accountancy market. Some might say he's giving away the secrets of Farnell Clarke's success, but that isn't the case. Will shares the same vision as I do – we want to see the rest of the UK accountancy market thrive and evolve. It's only through sharing experiences of what works – and, importantly, what doesn't work – that accountants will be able to keep up with the new demands they face.

This book is a perfect guide to firms wanting to take their digital 'first steps' and start their evolution. It isn't an overnight fix, so I expect the pages of this book to be well thumbed as accountants implement chapter by chapter to build their digital firm. But what happens once that's done?

Will's firm has always been an early adopter of technology, and the firm continues to be. Evolution isn't a destination, rather a continuous journey. What will the accountant's role look like post-MTD in a world underpinned by distributed ledgers, where bots and artificial intelligence undertake the majority of today's tasks? Well, there are many varying views (including a few of my own), but I can assure you Will and his firm will be at the forefront of the next age of technology, further sharing their experience with the rest of the market. I for one look forward to reading the next instalment in the digital evolution of accountants!

Steve Cox, IRIS

Introduction

. . . .

I'm not your typical accountant. I'm an entrepreneur who's passionate about giving great service and finding radical solutions to provide value and establish efficiencies. That involves using the best tech and sharing information freely. I'm great at the big picture, enjoy working on strategy and I'm not good at detail. I have a great team who are good accountants and we complement each other in terms of skills, orientation and character. Had I been a really good technical accountant, Farnell Clarke would not be the company it is today, and it would certainly not have grown by 36% year-on-year for a decade.

Early adoption of the best tech available, working towards internal and external processes that are as consistent, seamless and pain-free as possible, and creating an organisation that's always looking for efficiencies has paid off handsomely, and I want to pass the knowledge on. Hopefully this book, which summarises what we've learned during our leading-and-occasionally-bleeding-edge adoption of end-to-end cloud computing, will help you maximise profit and minimise pain in your firm's conversion to cloud accounting, helping you ensure future compliance with the currently nebulous requirements of MTD and facilitate your business's success in this new competitive environment.

Faced with important challenges in compliance practice and accounting services over the coming decade; including digital compliance requirements, AI and clients with an increasingly cloud-based digital approach to information processing, firms have to change to survive. I think going fully digital is the only logical choice.

Obviously this book is based primarily on my experience, so if the text is not attributed to anyone else, you can take it that it's me. But because I want to give you the best possible choices, I've brought in experts to give a more vendor-neutral balance. A lot of this book is my opinion, but we're not perfect, so I thought it would help to include my own mistakes.

Each chapter starts with a summary section, some bullet points and a little about what the entire chapter is about. My intent in creating this structure is to provide senior managers with a quick overview and the confidence that what follows is worth passing on to their staff. After that comes the body of the chapter and a tiny summary at the end. Throughout the book you'll see I've shared our experiences at Farnell Clarke, and to give more balance I've included extra case studies too.

If you have feedback on the ideas in this book, experience that adds value or questions that arise from it, it would be great to hear from you.

Will Farnell, Farnell Clarke

Chapter 1

Future-proofing and predictions

· ·

W e live in interesting times. Accounting and bookkeeping, effectively unchanged for hundreds of years, are undergoing a massive transformation. The extent to which a firm wants to adapt to meet challenges inherent in the current and changing landscape should directly relate to their client base, their service offerings, their flexibility and where appropriate, their exit strategy. But before we can start thinking about that, it's important to set the scene.

Why is future-proofing important?

- New disruptive firms have entered the accounting market. They're using re-engineered processes and new technology to provide cheap basic services.
- Other new tech-enabled firms are set up to offer greater value services.
- While MTD in its entirety has been set back, the portion relevant to VAT accounting is set. Firms that haven't taken this into account will have inefficiencies that reduce their competitiveness and profitability.
- Millennials, who will form 75% of the workforce and a sizeable proportion of clients by 2025, have a different set of expectations and lifestyle priorities that cannot be met by traditional firms.
- Even without current incentives to develop a fully digital practice, it's normal for manual accounting operations to take more than double the time of those using technology.
- Capturing and gathering data enables the offering of more timely, flexible advisory services.

But there's more

MTD gives us a reason for us to give clients for changing our services. This, combined with the requirements of an increasingly millennial client base is a big incentive for us to update our offerings, deepen our relationships with our clients and lay down foundations for a thriving practice over the coming years.

For me, though, the biggest reason is it's what our clients want!

And that's the hook, the thing that made me strive to automate as much as possible and help our clients do the same from the start of my practice. Since my firm's early days in 2008, I've constantly asked myself: 'What does the client want?' It's worked for us, and it's still working – our client retention is incredibly high. Our clients like knowing where they stand and they trust us to adopt only the tech that provides the best, most current, value-added fixed-price service we can.

MTD (Making Tax Digital) is the catch-all name given to the UK Government's plan to have compliance data communications completely digital. HMRC's eventual goal is to have all business transactions recorded as close as possible to the time when the transaction occurred. Eventually, quarterly reports (as opposed to annual reports) will be required. This is part of a worldwide movement to digitise tax collection, and governments everywhere are reforming burdensome tax compliance procedures. Costa Rica, Indonesia, Malaysia, Peru, Vietnam and Zambia are among the first to have adopted systems with some automated features while Brazil appears to be one of the leaders in digitising tax compliance.

This Chapter

We'll examine the ins and outs of this in detail throughout this book, but context is important. That's why this chapter discusses;

- the state of play of thought leadership and innovation in accounting.
- why MTD is a facilitator.
- trends that affect accountants everywhere, and
- the digital practice and why it's important to take action and future-proof our firms now rather than to wait.

Innovation and thought leadership

Like it or not, we're experiencing a situation of near overload with regards to thought leadership. Software vendors, for example, are throwing so much thought leadership in the market that it's reached a point where it's a required part of our brief to keep abreast of new thinking so that we can better serve our clients. There are both ethical and pragmatic reasons why we have to let our clients know what's changing in the market. But that doesn't mean everyone must follow all the advice. Far from it! We need to be selective and find people (or ideas) that offer answers only to the extent that we make sure we're innovating and getting the best value for our clients.

> **Innovative is *the* new term, replacing the buzzword proactive**

Some thought leaders are beginning to suggest firms take on innovation directors, and should figure out how that role should fit into current firm structures. My personal view is that such a role is beyond IT, and that it underpins everything that we should be doing as a business.

An analogy for the accountancy industry

These days it's nearly impossible to earn a living as a photographer because everyone takes their own images on the phone. It's all easier, you don't have to understand photography or be a photographer to take a photo, and the tech makes things look better. The press sends out reporters with iPhones more often than photographers. The same is true for the accountancy industry. Take Receipt Bank. Someone used to make a living keying in accounting software. Now you just photograph it and the data is entered. You don't even need to understand accountancy and there is a whole debate about whether or not we need to be employing qualified accountants for 30% of what we do. The point is that photographers still exist and so do accountants, but both need a different attitude and approach or they're unlikely to survive.

Innovation is about people, process, technology and far more. It's important to ask ourselves how we make sure that we're innovating and that we're getting the best outcomes. We need to ask ourselves constantly how we innovate so our external messages and communications are better than anyone else's. I think innovation is *the* new term, replacing the buzzword 'proactive'. While every firm used to say 'we are a proactive firm of accountants', the big buzzword is now 'innovative'. But what do those words actually mean?

For sure, the word 'innovation' reflects a shift of both thought and emphasis. First and foremost, we're still accountants, and our first objective is to keep our clients compliant. Every accounting firm in the country has the same key CSFs (critical success factors) to file accounts on time, get them right and help the client manage their tax position. If we get that wrong we have no business. What has changed

– the shift – is that we can see we'll come to a point where simply managing for compliance and tax position is not enough.

Some people have already realised this. As technology allows fresh players into the market, individuals are re-engineering the core functions of an accounting practice and some have designed really effective processes. Some tech companies and firms have used process consultants, process business analysts and more to get new software to perform traditional processes faster and smarter than everyone else. Just as Amazon has transformed the high street, these new disruptive tech firms pose a significant risk to older, more traditional practices. We ignore them at our peril.

CASE STUDY
Crunch: Study of market disruption

Crunch was set up in 2009 to offer low-cost accounting services through quite revolutionary technology. Back then it seemed that the company, which provided a no-frills service to contractors, was managed by non-accountants. They have done this very well, through the use of really slick systems and processes. Of course the company employs accountants too, but clients talk to relationship managers rather than old-style accountants. Their website claims they have grown into a top-100 accountancy firm in just a few short years.

You'll have to have had your head in the sand not to notice a new breed of entrepreneurial accountant around. They run firms on one pitch, and one pitch only – that they can deliver premium-priced services more effectively and for less money. They've exploited an opportunity to develop a cost-leadership model and build the slickest, most cost-efficient way to keep people compliant. But this isn't the only model in town. Some clients don't want that, because they know the cheapest model offers least and might not be sustainable. Those clients want more.

> **It's important to understand what such clients perceive as value so we can deliver it**

That desire – to get more from your accountant – is a significant business driver. Some clients will always value a relationship with a firm along that allows them to turn up and sit down, face-to-face with someone for a meeting. These clients will never be influenced by cost leaders – or, if they are, it'll only be peripherally. It's important to understand what they perceive as value so we can deliver it.

So, while compliance is a given, if we want to avoid being in a commoditised market space we have to say what else we do that differentiates us.

Do we deliver services that are 'better' or 'different'? Do we provide additional HR options (an easy one to offer)? Do we offer aspiring clients the opportunity to raise finance? It's important to be clear about who we are, who our clients are, who we want our clients to be and what we would like our future to look like – and to understand how to compete with these new disruptive low-cost compliance 'shops'. Beyond being the cost leader, we need to differentiate, we need something that enables us to be different. That enables us to guide clients' expectations away from time-based charging.

> ## APIs that can allow the bolting on of other products have taken cloud accounting to a whole new level

We're more likely to retain current and future clients if clients understand the extra value we provide. But the industry has an expectation that clients who are only getting 'keep out of jail' services are more likely to move to the lowest-cost offerings. If this is all your firm is concentrating on, it may be at risk.

And here's a thing I've discovered – when we start a meaningful conversation with our clients about what else we could do, they are universally surprisingly receptive!

That's because there's already an element of trust between us. That means that, with the right relationship and timely data, our clients would come to us first with every business question they have. We might not currently be able to deliver the answer every time, but with planning this could happen.

> ## With the right relationship and timely data our clients would come to us first with every business question they have. We might not currently be able to deliver the answer every time, but with planning this could happen

Future predictions and future-proofing

At its most fundamental level, before we adopted Receipt Bank, our clients were pretty relaxed about getting their records in. We would receive and process data that was 18 months old at best and two-and-a-half years old at worst. What value is it to anyone if we realise someone's exceeded a VAT threshold nine months after it's happened?

What is Receipt Bank?

Receipt Bank software extracts and organises key information from a client's receipts and invoices. It links directly to cloud software, thereby minimising manual data input and consequential errors.

So, bringing Receipt Bank on board and the absolute level of transparency that came with it made a whole load of sense.

Nowadays, new products are even more sophisticated, and APIs that allow developers to bolt on other products have taken cloud accounting to a whole new level – particularly since we started. Receipt Bank and GoCardless were the first add-on products we used, but the change since has been phenomenal.

Judging by what's happened over the last five years, the accounting market landscape will be unrecognisable in another five years' time. We've

What is GoCardless?

A simple direct debit solution that enables organisations to take recurring payments however and whenever they want to. This seamlessly integrates with online cloud accounting software.

seen the cloud evolve, but the huge change in accounting since 2008, when we became a cloud based practice, will pale into insignificance. Even if MTD is pushed back by the entire five years, developments in AI, machine learning and technology will transform what we deliver and how we manage the process. This is a very data-driven exercise, especially when it comes to managing data in QuickBooks, Payroll and all the other potential applications.

What is an API?

An API is a set of clearly specified functions and procedures that allow other organisations to access the features or data in an app, operating system, other program or service. By allowing access they are allowing other developers to create products that will bolt on or work with those features or data.

A while ago, during a long chat with the people at Xero, it transpired that any future technology change – whether MTD, blockchain or anything else – will be far easier if you get your processes in place now.

Meanwhile, to ensure that firms are compliant with the VAT reporting element of MTD they need to ensure that they're planning at least a year in advance,

because changing platforms halfway through your financial year (which is what will happen if they don't implement a solution now) is not the best option.

My conclusions, therefore, are that spotting trends is an important aspect of the service we should provide. Finding thought leadership to help with that is fine, but we should be able to keep in touch and follow developments too. While different people, industries and firms will spot and adopt trends at different times and for different reasons, the only safe way to future-proof our organisations is to adopt a fully digital practice.

The only safe way to future-proof our organisations is to adopt a fully digital practice

What does a digital practice look like?

These days all practices, big and small, use some kind of digital assistance or facilitation, and the extent to which it is automated or in the cloud is pretty much up to the businesses' decision makers.

To illustrate the difference between running accounts in the cloud and having your entire workflow in the cloud, let me tell you about one of the firms I've just talked to:

CASE STUDY
Will Farnell on costing manual and automated processes

After an initial discussion and high-level investigation with a large multi-partner firm in the UK, it became clear that this firm was very compliance-oriented and end-of-year focused. We then examined how this firm's clients delivered their accounts and broke this into different approaches (different types of software, the extent of fully manual processes and everything in between). During conversations with staff we established it took at least twice as long to do a manual records job as it did when the records had been digitised – irrespective of whether this was desktop, cloud or even spreadsheet!

So, the most important question was whether the firm reflected this disparity in their fees, or whether it was simply taking the more traditional approach of charging a fixed cost to prepare annual accounts and file the tax return. It was important to consider whether or not that fee flexed, and the repercussions if it didn't.

In my experience, in many cases the fee does not flex.

From this, we were able to consider the following:

If it takes one day to do computerised records and two days to do manual records, how many manual days are you doing each year? Working on the basis that every manual account is one lost workday, if you have 100 totally manual clients you have 100 days of inefficiency. This translates as lost profit or lost revenue, depending on where you want to position it.

This become a straightforward argument for digital systems versus manual ones, although consideration must also be given to the quality of the records.

From that, we can check whether the cloud or the desktop is a better fit for the client.

In this case there might not have been significant financial benefit, but the intangible benefit is clear – the client can continue to work on the cloud-based version in what is near enough real time. Even if we accept there is no financial gain, the process becomes more straightforward when everyone's working on the same ledger, we are all working on the same dataset, and we have confidence that nobody is working on an outdated version.

The biggest issue

The biggest barrier to providing new efficiencies and services is the focus on the once-a-year annual accounts. After that, if we do the client's bookkeeping for them we are no longer dependent on the client completing their data entry (and attendant accuracy challenges, because technology isn't subject to human error). By doing this we also get the benefits of planning our workflow better. More importantly, since we want to work with the client all year round, we need up-to-date data to enable us to look for other services to deliver and be delivering existing services more efficiently. We can only do this once we control the data.

> **Since we want to work with the client all year round, we need up-to-date data**

Exit strategy considerations

Firms don't have to be fully digital to survive. It's likely that a firm can do enough to get by with MTD. But how can such firms be sure in advance that they're doing enough?

If your exit strategy is to get out soon, and you have sufficient goodwill and clients to attract a future buyer, doing nothing might just work. However, if you want a viable, sustainable business, it won't. You'll be overtaken by everyone else doing it smarter with digital practices.

It's your choice, of course. But I believe that doing nothing will see you go out of business.

What does *'doing it smarter'* mean?

Smarter work is about utilising the efficiencies a firm can get by working in the cloud in ways that increase efficiency, save time and help provide focussed advisory to the client. A collateral benefit is the paperless or near-paperless office.

'We don't do anything with post, all we do is scan it and save it. I am sure there are still practices that have bits of paper and files, but, these days, why?'
Simon Edrich, AccountsCo

- No paper = savings in storage space.
- You can access your clients' data immediately, produce reports almost immediately and give extra value.
- Because so much can be automated, you can take on more work.
- Because the clients' data is immediately to hand, you can provide useful, timely services that might not previously have been cost effective or would have been too late to be truly useful.
- You can streamline your own internal processes as well as providing better, deeper client services.
- You can spend more time with more clients, developing a deeper relationship and becoming an essential part of their decision-support process.
- You can reduce the horrendous prospect that you might have to do your work twice to comply with pending MTD VAT (and later tax) rulings.
- You can create an environment that engages new staff and encourages them to stay and grow with you.

And finally

The reason given for MTD is to collect the right amount of tax, because too much tax revenue is currently lost through errors. Using higher levels of automation and more sophisticated software inevitably reduces the likelihood of complications, and passes off accurate details of compliance to government regulators. MTD is a massive catalyst and opportunity for firms to re-engineer and redesign their business, while also providing a justification for the clients to do so, since changes can be blamed on the government. Firms that see MTD as a way of moving to the cloud and turning off unwanted or complicated desktop software, and of changing everything they do, will benefit hugely.

Farnell

+

Clarke

=

accountancy

Chapter 2

Compliance is dead, so what's the strategy?

· ·

Once we've made the choice about whether or not to become a completely digital practice then we need to ask ourselves: what does it look like? How bold will the practice be? How ambitious? What's the endgame? What resources are available? In this we have two options: to do nothing and bury our heads in the sand, or to decide on survival and adapt for it.

Everyone tells us we have to be advisors, but advising what? The word means different things to different people. Most firms already call themselves advisors without necessarily defining what they advise, or what a client is – even when the client asks them! The digital firm needs to be clear on what we are going to advise, on how we propose to do it, and how to communicate this to existing and future clients. From that, we can work out whether we have the skill set to do what we're planning, and if we don't, we can investigate how to acquire it. Whether it is partnering with someone, changing equipment or tech, bringing in technologists instead of out-and-out accountants, or whatever is most appropriate to our firm and its plans.

Four important pointers in the development of a new service strategy

- Whether the increasing pace of change is advantageous or detrimental to our firms will have a direct result on the choices we make as we adapt.
- Compliance will soon be so well automated that our clients will look to other services for their value.
- We need to understand our data to develop new client services and improve our internal processes.
- As technology changes, so will our practice, and with it the skills we need.

But there's more

OK, compliance won't die and will remain fundamental to our services. But as it is further automated, the perceived value of the service will change, and potential revenue will be squeezed. We need to develop new product or service lines to replace this revenue – and sooner rather than later.

This Chapter

The rest of this chapter examines the impetus in developing a new strategy and approach for our firm, and the way we have been thinking about it.

> **We have to start looking at what it is we're actually doing. And that's not selling minutes in a day any more, but an outcome**

It's fine to say that historically accountants should simply instruct clients that they should change software (such as moving from Sage 50 – the mainstay of the 90s and 00s accounting software – to Sage One, Xero or QuickBooks) but that would have them missing an opportunity. By considering future likely MTD requirements, firms can stop using software that doesn't integrate with anything else and start using the cloud. Just changing tech isn't enough in the long term. Only changing the business model will stop firms being left behind.

Start looking again

It's not even because the clients are going to catch us out, as you'll read in the chapter *From APIs to Xero and beyond*.

Looking back, compliance became a focus because it got so complicated. Over the last 20 years in the UK, the institution of self-assessment created 31 January deadlines. Then RTI was introduced and everything else that came along meant an almost constant change in the way that compliance has been dealt with. So, it's not surprising that's what clients cared about and what they most needed help with. For a long time, making sure accounts complied with the latest laws, regulations and requirements meant there wasn't time for very much else. Go back to before this happened, to before relationships with clients were changed by compliance pressures, and accountants delivered more. Technology has now given us back that time, so we now have to look at how we can regain those deep-rooted relationships with clients where they can't imagine having a business without an accountant as an advisor, sounding board, and more.

The problem for firms adopting that approach is that the underlying business model must change. How do you adopt pricing models to deal with the pressure on compliance fees, and to adopt more advisory roles? That most firms don't have the required skill set is something I'll examine in the chapter *If you build it they will come*. Meanwhile, if we accept that firms need to become advisors, we need to think differently.

So, if we accept that compliance is being automated and we can't survive being a compliance firm, we have to replace the compliance revenue. This means reversing the downwards trend that links service cost, value, and time recording, and wanting to bill by the hour because the tech makes the job more efficient. So you have fewer hours and therefore less revenue. Once you get over that hurdle, you can consider what you do to replace.

Demonstrating value and preserving income

We need to think about income preservation. We know we're going to lose this income because we're not charging by the hour any more, and losing 80% of our revenue isn't clever. The client gets exactly the same value before or after automation, so we have to start looking at what it is we're actually doing. And that's not selling minutes in a day any more, but an outcome – whatever that might be. If we can deliver the outcome to our clients faster than we used to, that doesn't reduce the value of our service, so we need to be prepared to defend that to clients and potential clients.

As tech replaces our compliance practice, we need to think about the services we want to provide and identify the skills we need to do it. Tech can't replace

> **We always need to nail core services first**

the human interaction, but if you just have this thing called compliance and only talk to your clients once a year, you need to find something else. We need to create more services as products, depending on our client requirements and using the data we already have – but, as James Kay says, we always need to nail core services first.

Generally, when talking to other firms, I start the conversation with this discussion and ask whether they accept there's downward pressure on fees. From there we talk about how automation will drive efficiency and effectiveness in the manner that firms have historically delivered products and services. Once a firm accepts that, and understands that tech's going to make their work processes more effective, I ask if they accept the need to replace some of the revenue that will inevitably be lost.

The next question is: how? How is this revenue going to be replaced? At the start they don't see many options. Some firms already provide a full service, with private finance management divisions, wealth management divisions, finance divisions, insolvency divisions, and other services they can sell. What about the everyday client who wants to make sure his home business won't go bust and set up a pension… but then what? I ask what other services are they going to deliver, and whether they've considered other ways in which they can support their clients.

So, what does the firm do with the freed-up time and utilities? This is where there's a great opportunity. Replacing the perceived value of compliance services, and actually delivering value by using compliance and the data behind it to deliver information that kick-starts new conversations with your clients. Such things help the client, and therefore help maintain fee levels, because you've replaced the perceived value of compliance with something else of value.

> **Changes in tech don't normally result in job losses, but rather in a change in the work that people do**

It's at this stage we need to discuss the whole bookkeeping issue. In the past it's been seen as low value and has been left to the clients, historically with desktop software. That's because it wasn't cost effective – it wasn't an easy thing to do without sending people out. Now, the first real value of the tech available today is to make bookkeeping a viable service line. However, it's more than that, because when you have that data, if you're updating it regularly, you're also in regular contact with the client. This is where you can start building relationships, learning enough about the client, their objectives and aspirations, to provide value in the future.

Of course it depends what the bookkeepers are doing. If your client's a small limited company or sole trader paying a nominal monthly fee, we can now provide an app and a pain-free way to record receipts, which means they don't need a bookkeeper. Bookkeepers therefore need to recognise this and adapt their offering, examining where they can add value to the client and move beyond charging for data entry. Studies have been done around automation and the data entry roles at risk, but, as we've seen with other tech such changes don't normally result in job losses, but rather in a change in the work that people do.

> **The client gets exactly the same value before or after automation**

> **'Having data is vital. It enables us to look to the future and make plans to allow us to achieve our goals.' James Kay**

Let's look at data

Client data is something with which we're all familiar, but the successful digital firm needs to be aware that other forms of data exist. Data from our own processes and efficiencies, from client business trends and competition, internal data, and data on how we interact with existing and future clients, partners and suppliers.

Collecting and analysing all available data is important for us, is because it helps us expose variability, optimise operations, understand how best to serve our clients, and more. Even if we're not yet going to do so, we need to find new ways to record such data, since examination of large amounts of it helps uncover hidden patterns and correlations that can create competitive advantage and result in more effective marketing and communications. That in turn will increase revenue.

CASE STUDY
Farnell Clarke
Why I set our strategy to be cutting edge from the start

Historically accountants go to university, leave, and then join a firm on some professional form of training contract. They learn how to be accountants, qualify, and either: stay where they are, do really well, become a partner, and continue to drive the firm the way they were taught; or they might leave the practice and go to industry taking their skillsets with them. This is a completely different environment and they are either lost to the practice, or will set up their own practice sometime in the future. Since they'll more than likely set up a firm in the way they were taught, nothing changes.

Double-entry bookkeeping was devised in the 1400s, and is still the same today. As a profession we're not that up for change. We've used the same processes, the same structures, and, when it arrived, the same software. Yes, of course it's evolved – from ledger to spreadsheet, to Sage and desktop publishing. Now we're going through the next step, from cloud technology to the digital firm for some, and from desktop to cloud technology for others.

When I set up my firm in 2007, most accountants did what they had been doing for the last 10 years. I had the benefit of having not been trained in that old way, so I had no preconceptions about what my practice should look like. I was able to think through how I'd like my accounting firm to look, and from the start I wanted to have no charge for ad hoc meetings and transparency on prices. At the time that was pretty novel.

At the same time, the internet was here, and we were comfortable with it. I thought there must be accounting products that one could use online. It took about 18 months before we found a product we thought was right. It wasn't called cloud-based at the time, but when we started working with KashFlow in 2008 it was online. To adopt it seemed a complete no-brainer. Why wouldn't we want access to client data 24/7? Why wouldn't we want access to the same ledger on which our clients were working? Having just one version of ledger has so many advantages. With this, it became possible to provide the type of bookkeeping services accountants have historically avoided. This gave us the opportunity to help clients process transactions, and to assist in decisions in a timely manner.

Providing for growth

I often hear about firms that aren't comfortable with the idea of taking on more clients, even if this is a direct result of needing to change to survive. For the fully digital firm this is much less of a concern. Growth is about scalability, and scalability is about digital transformation. Above all it's important to recognise technology is an enabler in the widest sense of the word. It's fine to say 'use Xero instead of Sage 50', but the biggest challenge is that firms have to understand that their underlying business model must change, and that automation means taking on more clients, which is a considerably easier process.

> If your firm is on a growth curve – which any firm can achieve – when you come to recruit it's really difficult. To avoid resourcing crunches, constantly look for people with a culture fit and when you find them, take them on, so that they're already in place as client numbers grow and you start really needing them.

How to ensure we can cope with more clients

- Partner with the best.
- Share knowledge and learning.
- Stay open to ideas, opportunities, business models and more.
- Ensure processes are seamless, transparent and repeatable.
- Keep staff updated.
- Understand and map how to transition clients.
- Understand how different client habits and processes hit the bottom line.
- Never settle for staff who aren't quite right.
- Ensure you have all the skills you need in the firm.
- Constantly look for ways to improve.
- Never stop recruiting; if you're on a growth curve never stop being open to finding good people.

And finally

Every firm is different, with different characters and clients. There's still time to differentiate yourself. Think to the future, and about more than compliance. To implement such changes, remember it's important to ensure the client's data is accurate, maintenance is timely and relationships are more than an annual compliance-based meeting. That means setting a strategy for development and knowing who your clients are – and who they're not – from the start.

Chapter 3

Efficiencies, fees and the client

· ·

L et me be clear: accountancy is changing. Billing by the hour is no longer an option when the client can clearly see the process of compliance is automated, so we need to change both our and our clients' expectations. The shift to advisory work is replacing income that will be lost, and it depends on us providing a better service to clients, ensuring we're responding to the changing market, and explicitly recognising that data entry and box ticking is likely to be replaced by robots. That's why I often say 'compliance is dead'. It's not, of course – I use it to grab attention – but the fact remains that while compliance will never die, we have to get our approach right. And for as long as we focus on selling commodities, our primary focus will be price sensitive, forced down by fully automated compliance-only shops, and our firms may die as a result. That's why we have to change our approach, and it's what I'm covering in this chapter.

The fact that we were providing a service nobody else was, using new tech, has been a key part of our growth, and at the point of publishing this book there's still an opportunity to be gained in moving quickly. In certain regions you'll find one or two firms who get it and are way ahead, but there's a big gap between those front-runners and the core pack, and there are some good niches to fill. And since the new digital practice utilises a mix of digital technology and digitally aware staff to deliver first-class services effectively and efficiently through maximum levels of automation, it's important to understand why we should drive these efficiencies.

There are a number of reasons firms need to utilise the efficiencies of automation in a different charging system:

- With MTD, HMRC are building towards a regulatory regime that will effectively penalise practices that have minimal automation, since for them compliance reporting at four or six times a year will be horrendously time consuming and who will pay?
- Waiting until HMRC requirements stabilise will lose practices their much-needed competitive edge and may make it harder to demonstrate compliance to new conduct risk management requirements.
- We need to build our practices so they attract millennials as both clients and staff, not least because 75% of our staff will be millennials by 2025.
- Proactive firms are already seeing MTD as a catalyst for transformation, which they'll use to offer a range of cost-effective services.
- The streamlining inherent in the digital practice enables us to consider new service lines, advisory services and management reporting, and this will enable our organisations to thrive in an increasingly competitive environment.

Conduct Risk

'For many sectors – and notably finance – the 'future of regulation' looks to be about better recognising and controlling so-called *'people factor risks'*. In economically developed countries all around the world, Conduct Risk regulators have started to rein in wayward senior managers through the use of new controls developed from the latest behavioural science insights.' **Dr. Roger Miles**

But there's more

I enjoy the fact that Farnell Clarke has always been an early adopter of quality tech, and I'm happy that the drive to MTD is a stimulus for us to provide considered and useful value-added services. But for me, the biggest reason we need to adopt new business models to support our strategy to remain a leading-edge fully digital firm is that it's what our clients want!

The more complex systems require a more intellectual input

This Chapter

This chapter looks at how efficiencies can be obtained, the way we've considered fees and how we communicate the change from time-based fees to advisory services with our clients.

Narrowing the gap

As I said in the chapter *Compliance is dead, so what's the strategy?*, if we accept compliance is being automated and that we can't survive being a solely compliance firm, we have to reverse the downward trend that links service cost, value, and time recording. I don't think we're there yet, but it will become increasingly important to use the economies of going digital to maintain competitiveness.

To drive our digital practice we need fast accurate access to our clients' data. And if the client has their own bookkeeper or does their own bookkeeping, this can become more problematic. So the first challenge for us is getting clients to change the way they see our charges and use our services.

> **Machine learning iterates towards the right answer but doesn't necessarily ensure you're actually going to get it**

A secondary challenge is that leading-edge firms – particularly those specialising in tech – will get the tech to make the process faster and more efficient, and will therefore be able to deliver a lower cost offering. This is where firms currently suspect they'll lose money, fearing their clients may perceive they can get the same value for less money for a very basic service – but in our experience that hasn't been the case.

There are two aspects to considering how to gain efficiencies: the accounting and the tax. Currently both require human expertise to get it right, so providing the data is entered correctly the systems will give you a pretty good first show. Then it's about reviewing it and thinking around it – that's where human input comes in. Anything out of the ordinary is a bit harder, and has to be reorganised to be in the system correctly. Different systems have different complexities, so the more complex systems require a more intellectual input.

In theory the tax codes should be fairly logical, so machines should be able to do it all – but they can't for now. I guess the thing with machine learning is that it iterates towards the right answer but doesn't necessarily ensure you're actually going to get it. Over a huge number of samples, machine learning may therefore give you more correct answers than a human, but for a complex company with clients needing you to get it right first time, human intervention will remain essential for a good while to come.

In the old days, the date, invoice number, description and normal attributes of an invoice are automatically recognised by systems. They're not quite there yet. Maintenance costs, indirect costs and invoices by a company for something unanticipated aren't going to be recognised by the machine. Obvious things like gas bills are straightforward, but the machine won't know whether Bob Smith and Son from down the road is a corner shop, and whether it is stationery or a sandwich being purchased though I'm sure that will come. Then again, eventually invoices will be coded to show where they should be posted. Then even the need for machine learning will have disappeared.

Getting fees right

Initially, after listening to the pricing gurus, I brought in an ex-managing partner of a mid-tier firm to give me a bit of support. He told me that if we had a conversation with our clients, explained why we needed to change the fixed fees, we wouldn't lose them. He was right, and I realised that, had I been able to go back and implement the technology we're now using, we would already have had a different practice. At the same time as this was happening, we decided to implement GoProposal, which I'll discuss more in the *APIs to Xero* chapter.

One of the major reasons for this is that it closed the opportunity for scope creep, which itself means we have a more logical pricing scheme. With just a little training we were able to set it up and start issuing proposals with it inside a day. We've set it up so it works in bands of turnover thresholds and transaction numbers, and we've had no big issues since.

Where clients were not paying the right fee, we started by reviewing our fixed fees and standing orders because we hadn't reviewed them for years. Before GoProposal, clients only got an additional invoice if they asked for another service. Some were fine, but on examination we realised we'd been over-servicing others all along. Since I brought James in as MD, fees are reviewed regularly.

Where clients were not paying the right fee, we explained this to them. We also told each client that, for example, we might bill them £250 for the year and put a discount line on the invoice, which would bring it down to £175 for that year. That set our expectations, but also added hugely significant additional fees straight on our bottom line. After a year, we went round a second time, and in many cases, removed the transition discount.

Showing your difference

Avoid giving the same message that everyone else is giving. Think about niche markets or whatever else gives you that differentiator or if you are a traditional firm, and your past USP (unique selling point) has been as a full service firm, or a mid-tier firm with access to lots of additional service lines, then how do you incorporate things, then how do you leverage that to get the value of the cloud alongside your market positioning?

Alongside that, a lot of firms have gone wrong by trying to create a sub brand for their bookkeeping business. This causes confusion, provides conflicting messages and the firm has made it very difficult for themselves to demonstrate value when they create a new brand. Clients still want guidance, and once you've positioned your services as cheap it will be difficult to change the message.

The vision: how bold do you want to be?

I think becoming a digital practice is the right thing to do. So if you decide you're going to become a digital practice, what does it look like? How bold do you want to be? How ambitious? What resources do you have and what do you want?

New business models, new people, new ideas

It's important to ask yourself where you sit in the market and whether you're prepared to leave your comfort zone. To do that, it's important to understand what the profile of the client base is, as it will influence their readiness for change. If you have an ageing client base, how are you going to attract the new business owners once the people you've been working with retire? Can the change be undertaken without alienating your existing client base? What sort of clients are you looking to retain? And what sort of clients might you be better off losing altogether?

I recently spoke with an Irish firm that saw an opportunity to be the first movers in their area. Because the concept of digital practice is at a very early stage, they see potential competitive advantage, but they also see themselves as a traditional firm. They told me they'd never be like our firm because there's an expectation to present themselves in a particular way. They're also unsure that they can go down the route of imposing one single process.

A key part of decision-making is deciding who you want to benchmark yourself against. Who's going to be your competition? You see, in the longer term each firm must look at the out-and-out digital practices as competition, because location is no longer a barrier. Anybody can set up an accounting firm and sign up with Xero or Intuit as a partner and deliver services very efficiently. That means the risk for old established firms is twofold: firstly, they may find themselves outpriced by firms in any other location; and secondly, their own staff, once trained, may see little opportunity for advancement and leave, because nowadays finding a new firm is very easy.

Paul Bullpit of Wow on developing a vision

People don't buy what you do, they buy why you do it. Customers who are business stakeholders have a really clear purpose. Don't talk about what you do, talk about why you do it and talk about what gets us out of bed in the morning.

Tackle the business, get it by going head-on. Have the vision. Reinforce it, build a platform, be really clear on the products and services you want to deliver, how you want to deliver on them and the product and services you want to use. Have a clearly defined idea of what you do and don't try to be all things to all people. Truth be told, apps probably don't change that fast, but getting the right ones is a constant iteration. A lot of people don't have this clear idea and they just deal with whatever comes through the door, what is thrown at them. I just don't see how you can build a business using three different online packages that all do the same thing. You can't be an expert in all of them, while if you use just one and stick to it you can achieve exponential results.

From great service to great customer experience

Early adopters have gone through the cycle of: firstly, delivering great services; secondly, incorporating great tech to continue delivering these great services (or the clients would have left); thirdly, using tech to extract a better quality of data for analysis; and finally, using all this to give great customer experience.

Of course you need to look at what your potential competition is delivering, how they're delivering it and how they charge. Since we're all delivering the same services we always have done, we have to be sure of where the value is delivered, where we can use efficiencies and tech to deliver our core services, and where this provides a wider choice of value-added services or gives more opportunity to deliver what we do.

It's not about reverse engineering for us – even though that's how Xero developed their app. It's a layering – now we can deliver our core business really effectively, we need to think about how we can develop our capacity to deliver really great additional services.

Information as a catalyst to value conversations

The first thing is that we have to have quality data that is up to date and relevant, to enable us to turn data into meaningful information. This becomes the catalyst for us to be able to add value by using the information to help clients, positioning our service according to what we know about clients' aspirations.

For your client, it's about the transition

Some existing clients use no software, some use desktop apps and some use other forms of cloud-based computing. To facilitate a digital practice, we need clients to understand that to get the data we need to help them deliver timely information, we first need to be able to access that data in a timely way. Our clients have understood this so far, even though most firms who haven't moved to a fully digital practice yet perceive this as the biggest challenge.

Some firms might see MTD as a revenue opportunity, but this is short-sighted. Another firm is bound to do basic no-frills compliance cheaper. Besides, can you really justify charging your clients for doing multiple submissions? Isn't it about using the transition to work smarter or more efficiently?

'I think we're catching a wave. People are seeing the competitive landscape changing. They know that they want to do something but haven't worked out what they want to do, why they should be doing it or how they should make the transition.' **Will Farnell**

CASE STUDY

Matt Flanaghan of BlueHub on the benefits of going fully digital

We're a client integrator, working with end users as well as firms. Our clients come to us either because Will's gauged their interest or they've discovered a need. Building close working relationships with accountancy practices is central to our business. We know the industry's changing and we've helped hundreds of practices develop their skills in cloud systems to create new revenue streams. We specialise in scoping and implementing cloud-based systems and supporting businesses through the process.

Our first conversation with the client is a kind of 'triage' call. It's actually a friendly interrogation of what they do. It isn't massively nitty-gritty – just about high-level processes. We're looking to see if we can satisfy their requirements and whether we feel we can work with them – and this in large part depends on valuing what they do and understanding the complexity of it. If a client wants a lot but isn't willing to invest, we know it won't work, so we try to make sure expectations are set correctly from the start. As part of the triage call we do something we call the PIA ('pain in arse' radar). This helps us understand how much work there might be and so we can change the pricing if needed. Client mentality feeds into that – those who look like they'll need a lot of help and will constantly question quality process issues more time spent and more cost to the project. The reason we can price reasonably well is we have battle scars.

From that we give them the next steps and the likely budget. We make sure they get value and some guidance from the call, irrespective of whether they stay with us, but at the end of the call it's about them saying yes or no. It's a very quick sales process.

We can estimate the amount of work from experience. We've tracked how long it takes and know by now. In the early days we would budget by time, but now 90% of the time we give a fixed price for the scope we're given.

I personally work in strategic work, getting clients ready for a transition when they have a thousand clients or more. That's important because data discipline across the accountancy sector is traditionally poor, and recent sector or other information might not be stored. I might be dealing with data strategy: for example, a thousand-client firm that hasn't kept its practice management system up to date with the right data to be useful. There are often challenges in identifying which clients are complex and which aren't. Data cleansing and updating takes time, but once it's done, the firm can make much more effective decisions about client transfers. Without this data, firms can get caught out by unexpected or previously unseen problems

> **The reason we can price reasonably well is we have battle scars**

while the work's well underway. This can obviously cause huge problems.

Complex clients need more planning, and good strategic knowledge of data enables the transfer to be proactive rather than reactive, so getting this right has enormous benefit to the client in terms of time, money and credibility.
Matt Flanagan

What about the costs?

It's true that extra costs are incurred in subscriptions, and many of the add-ons cost a little extra, but I believe the advantages to your clients and your practice far outweigh these costs.

GoProposal and client efficiencies

A lot of users we engage with are finding that, because of the way data is presented back to clients, they are selling at much higher rates than before. That's because GoProposal gets you to think of the little things that might just have been thrown in. By giving its users the mindset of applying a price to each action or product, it ensures things don't get missed. An example is that we never used to charge clients for using our office address. We thought it was quite useful for the paperwork to come direct to us so that we could deal with it. But that's a service, as it means that clients' personal addresses need not be made available on public records, and there's a value to that.

One of the challenges of fixed-fee pricing is there's an element of assumption – *a hunch* – on arriving at the fees in the first place. And now, in a number of cases, GoProposal is delivering higher prices than our hunch. It's great, because we can use the system to ensure measurable and transparent consistency.

We have expectations based on output. For example, there's an additional cost for the production of more than three monthly payslips. Each GoProposal proposal demonstrates to the client that there is a level of structure and science behind the fees, which is important as we demonstrate value while moving away from time-based invoicing.

'I suppose there are always exceptions, such as when clients suddenly call and say 'I need a mortgage application filled in, so need my end of year accounts doing tomorrow'. I would hate anyone to lose a house – I know how that feels – but it's a hard call because we already have our work assignments. We've toyed with charging more for priority service, so if the client's year end is April and they ask for the accounts on 1 May I think it's fair to charge more. Then once the accounts are done the personal tax return needs to be done as well, of course. It's the knock-on effects that get you. But back to the mortgage. If we can't do accounts, we'll produce management information, in which case I'd probably just do them without charging – provided the data was up to date.' **Frances Kay**

'We've effectively developed an additional menu-style price list that might include costly forecasts, payroll for significant numbers of people, share-structure services, new starters and leavers, closing companies. The kind of things that become significant over time.' **James Kay**

Ingredients for success

Xero suggests there are four factors that lead to positive outcomes and higher growth for accounting firms, and – with certain qualifications – I agree. But I'd add a fifth:

1. Proactively transitioning desktop clients online

2. Numbers

I think the most important point here isn't directly related to economies of scale, but most accountants generate new business through referral. The more clients you have, the more clients you can get. Looking for the trigger for all the referrals to us, I believe an important aspect was that five or six years ago we had tech that nobody else had. The larger the number of online accounting clients you have, the larger the pool of potential referrals, but more than that, with a larger pool of online clients you have a stronger case when you tell people *'this is how I do it'*. Given that the majority of firms still aren't working in the cloud, there's still time to utilise the opportunity to show how you're doing something that others might not do.

> **Getting the right staff in the right place with the right training at the right time is vital to your future success**

3. Economies of scale

Of course economies of scale come into play when you have a conformity of workflow and process. Clients know what to expect, budgeting is easier, and as some of the pressure is taken from the year end, we have the time as accountants to provide value-added services.

There's an argument that one member of staff can service far more clients because they are spending less time keying data. If it takes five minutes per client per day instead of an intense period of work at month end, we spread our work over a period of time and are likely to have far more confidence in the quality and timeliness of the data.

4. Client time

Firms that spend more time with clients and less time with spreadsheets generate between two and eight times more revenue per employee. This opportunity to get involved in advisory and relationship management is exciting. You have to find time to work out what services you will build in, and time to get to know the client better. By understanding the pressures on the client and their pain points, and by combining this with knowledge of their short-, medium- and long-term objectives, you can find more ways to support them.

5. Consistent HR

Getting the right staff in the right place with the right training at the right time is vital to your future success. They need to be engaged with your clients, see a clear career progression, want to stay with your firm and to add value to your clients.

And finally

Clients are going to recognise the increasing transparency of fees in the market. With more and more firms publishing their fees on their websites, how do you make your clients 'stickier'? How do you make them as happy as possible? How can you maintain margins if the pressure of fees is also there? Is there a better way of working with your clients? For example, as a sole trader, can you actually work with just 25 clients, deliver a far deeper service and earn the same money?

As a firm committed to using leading-edge tech, Farnell Clarke's MO is to continually search for new ways to provide value to our clients. We are not alone in this approach, and have talked to a number of traditional firms who take the view that radical change is vital. They've decided the old way of working is no longer viable and have reviewed and changed the strategy, sometimes subsequently running their organisation as if it was a different sort of business entirely.

While keeping clients out of jail will always be our fundamental responsibility, our clients don't care about compliance. That means we need to get to a point where we can do compliance for free, building on the process to offer services that our clients value and the proactive relationship management that goes with it.

I'm an

~~Accountent~~

~~Accounttent~~

~~Accountint~~

I'm good

with maths

Chapter 4

If you build it, they will come

Using business culture and environment to recruit the best

. . . .

We've been growing fast. Like everyone, once our underlying business model changed, we needed to get the right staff. At 36% year-on-year we've also had to move offices several times. More on that in the chapter *Migrating to a fully digital cloud practice*. Even with the right tech (a great enabler), repeatable transparent business processes and a great team, we have our eye out for more people. And we're looking for millennials, because of their approach and because we're looking to attract clients who relate to them. With great competition for good accountants throughout the market, you need to create a culture that attracts, retains, trains and motivates the people you want. Beyond this, it makes sense that engaged and satisfied employees feel a better connection with their company and are driven to help their employers – and their clients – succeed. However, the millennial generation are digital natives and often aren't motivated by the things you'd expect, so working out the best way to attract them takes some thinking.

How to create an attractive office culture

- **Establish core values and goals**
  Not just team goals – incorporate personal goals too.

- **Good career progression**
  Brainstorm with them what they think it takes to succeed, show you're listening and come up with something that reflects the values and suggestions in words they use.

- **Make people feel appreciated**
  Provide flexible working, and time, if possible. Allow employees to work from home, and give regular reviews and 360s. More than this, brainstorm the social media stuff and client pain points and empower them to suggest and write appropriate social media pieces. See the chapter *Content marketing for the digital firm*.

- **Create fun work spaces**
  Making the office a nice environment is important. Consider décor, plants, outside space, and ask them what they'd like. We went the extra mile by adding a pub-themed meeting room – complete with beer and a pool table – but whatever you do, consider team building and morale.

- **Plan team events**
  This is not a huge challenge when you have a pub on the premises! But try sports or a breakfast club or delegate the organisation to team members.

- **Consider volunteering**
  Encourage or incentivise your staff. Think of charity runs, walks or helping others.

But there's more

As a firm known for embracing the cloud, the idea of being a digital practice goes beyond technology. Culture plays an important role. Tech-savvy people want to work in different environments, and they have different ideas about what they want to do and how they're going to do it. The trick, therefore, is to work out what makes your firm special and how to show this to the staff you want to attract.

This Chapter

Recruitment isn't simple. We've learned to hire only people who really will fit our culture, and have come to our approach through the management of an excellent MD (James Kay, a key non-millennial we recruited to fill skills gaps in our management). There's always work to do, and always ways we can do things better for our staff, our clients and our potential clients. And now we've achieved a workplace culture that attracts the type of staff and client we want, we're on permanent lookout for new candidates for our team.

Here we share some of the things we – and others – have done to develop an attractive company culture that you might use as a starting point.

Express yourself

Back when I first started the business, people would ask what I did. I'd say, 'I'm an accountant, but I'm not your typical accountant.' That became our strapline, and part of our ethos. I'm not good at detail – I have a great team who are good accountants. If I was a really good technical accountant, this business wouldn't be like this. I brought on Frances as co-director, and at first I was of the impression that she was all the things I wasn't. Well, it turned out that far from complimentary, our outlooks were nearly identical. This left a massive void in our management structure – we could do the great big picture and network stuff, but struggled with system and process stuff.

We decided to do some skills profiling to understand what type of person we needed. We applied the Insights Discovery personality test for our management team. We looked at what we did, where each aspect of our skills sat in their colour code and what that meant. That enabled us to identify gaps we needed to fill.

'Will and I had a strategic planning meeting together outside the office. We examined what we wanted, particularly our weaknesses and instantly knew we couldn't fill the gaps. Will knew James from some of our socials, and suggested I speak to him before he invited him to join the company. As James is my husband he wanted to make sure it was right.' Frances Kay, Co-Director.

As a result we recruited James, whose skills sit nicely in the middle of the gap. Now I work with James (as MD) and Frances as co-director overseeing the onboarding process and welcome teams. This means I can concentrate on the big picture stuff – business development, new technology and strategy.

'Will and I often find ourselves disagreeing over something. It's par for the course. I respect and rely on his technical ability and the knowledge he has built up over the years and I think he respects the fact that I know all my staff very well so we don't generally clash.' **James Kay**

The Insights Discovery System

The Insights Discovery system is a profiling system run by Iridium Consulting. It can used in a variety of different applications, including individual development, team development, leadership development, sales, recruitment and selection. Each individual's profile is generated from the results of a quick online 25-question questionnaire, and Iridium can then provide feedback, training or advice along with a highly detailed personalised profile.

CASE STUDY
Paul Bulpitt; on finding the right staff

At The WOW company we have people of all ages, and the degree to which people offer great services and to which they adopt new tech doesn't correlate with their age. I wouldn't want to be pigeon holed as a generation, it's not fair on millennials to do the same thing. We're looking for people that our culture fits. At The WOW company the biggest thing we did a good few years ago was get an external consultant to codify our values. We knew it had 5 key concepts. Leadership, connection, making a difference, creativity and innovation and fun.

All of a sudden we had a really clear idea of what made someone a good fit for us - there can be a tendency to say they're tech strong or good with clients, but actually we need someone who is strong in these five values. If you're not strong on those, you're not going to survive or thrive at WOW.

Look ahead!
Why millennials are important

Millennials will become the majority of our workforce sooner rather than later. They'll bring in new customers and ultimately will be more in touch with the generation that follows them. We need staff who think like our target customers, and so we need new ways to attract and keep them as we embrace new technologies and platforms, drive strategic business advantages and stay ahead of the competition.

Collateral benefits of the right environment

'Before the refit we were in very beige boxy offices in small and quite depressing rooms. Refurbishing the office a while ago made my life easier. There was an immediate direct benefit in recruitment, and the press we got – online and in print – helped our big push on promoting ourselves. On the back of that we got approached by a lot of people who wanted to work here. James and I both brought relationships with a lot of agencies, but they're very expensive. Now we get a lot of speculative applications, things have become considerably easier.'
Frances Kay

Look for the right mindset

I talk a lot about the millennial generation and give them a heavy focus – particularly with regards to new client accounts. Most of our core accounts team are millennials, and we've found the evolution of attitudes with regards to tech very interesting – 20-year-olds have never known it another way. For them the app-driven culture is the norm, while for the rest of us it can feel a bit like we're living in *Star Trek*.

We've built our culture and values around those people, and clients are attracted to firms that employ people they identify with. That said, I think of myself as a millennial – certainly I have many of the traits – and a good number of our clients and colleagues, while not technically fitting into the age range, behave as millennials would. We've built the business so we can have engaging conversations with these people.

As I said, people look for an accountant to mirror themselves. That's because we all need to feel that the people we work with understand what we're trying to do. Positioning ourselves for that market is not just a matter of branding – it transfers into everything else we do. Our staff need to understand tech because our leading use of tech is a key part of what makes us different.

Culture is an important component when building a practice

Take a big organisation like Google as an example. What we see from the outside is a vibrant and flexible culture. Does this vibrant culture automatically translate into more productive staff? As outsiders we assume so. Can a similar approach be translated to a professional services firm? That's a question I've asked myself, and I decided it can. We have a pub – well, a pub-themed meeting room complete with beer and a pool table and brightly coloured walls – in our nice light offices, and while I'd hope this atmosphere encourages more productivity, at the very least it expresses a sense of our identity and what we're trying to do as a firm for clients and staff.

Having a fun work environment shows we don't take ourselves too seriously, and that we're here for our clients. But what's really important is that there is a correlation between how clients perceive the firm and the working environment of that firm. You can't run something that doesn't match the brand image without a mismatch that clients will pick up on.

> **At the very least it expresses a sense of our identity and what we're trying to do as a firm for clients and staff**

What is culture?

To understand and communicate our firm's culture, we need to think about our purpose. For more on this see *Compliance is dead, so what's the strategy?, Efficiencies, fees and the client, and Content marketing for the digital firm* and the things we love about it. Among my favourite things about Farnell Clarke are: the people; that the firm's at the leading edge; that we're able to help others benefit from our experience; that we have great communication with our clients; that we're transparent; and that we charge fixed fees for great services.

Once we understand our culture, we need to communicate it. What makes working in this firm different? But it's not enough to just *tell* people what our culture, ethics and principles are. We need to *live* them and practice them daily, working with our staff to improve and refine what makes us who we are. All aspects of this are important – and, incidentally, can go into our social media marketing plan once we've decided on and reviewed them.

> It's not enough to just *tell* people what our culture, ethics and principles are. We need to *live* them and practice them daily

Once we've established our culture and documented our process, we not only have a way of communicating our cultural essence to others, but also of obtaining and taking basic measurements and communicating in ways that will contribute towards future improvements. Such metrics can also help us understand how to be resilient and flexible in the face of the future tech changes that we all know will come.

This isn't something we can just decide on, implement and leave. The idea of a company culture needs to be defined and revisited. Not with huge and complex documents, but by consideration and periodic discussion.

CASE STUDY
Grant Smith of Armstrong Watson on recruitment and skillsets

When we started this journey there were a lot of rose-tinted glasses. Apps were selling the dream and there was a lot of speculation as to what freed staff would do. But the type of people we need is different now. We need people who can train clients on Xero and use a lot of the app integrations. Such abilities and attitudes require a different skill set and it's is more easily found from a younger generation. We don't want to lose valuable people who have 30 years of loyalty and experience. To bring them up to the more technical levels requires significant training, more interaction with customers and some won't like this. It's a challenge.

'Recruitment seems to have always been a headache for practitioners. As chewed over in a recent AccountingWEB Any Answers thread, a staff member's poor performance can have a knock-on effect on the whole firm, with deadlines not met, client complaints, work piling up and HR entanglement. But with the profession in the grip of a skills shortage, what can a hard-pressed firm do?'
Richard Hattersley, AccountingWEB

Making our culture special

Back in 2016, for the first time in our fairly short history, we lost quite a lot of staff. We found it difficult to recruit replacements because of competition from other regional firms. While we could truthfully say we do some really cool stuff here, it wasn't reflected in the work environment, so we refitted the office to reflect what we were doing. This generated the desired effect, resulting in an increase of interest and a flow of better quality candidates – which is important. I know I've said it before but people want to identify with their accountants, and with the new staff came more millennial businesses.

> For a long time we were constantly trying to catch up, and were unable to make best use of the data and our new client relationships because there simply wasn't time

Case study introduction

Our rapid growth meant we were always desperate for staff. At the beginning we had no formal, repeatable staff processes. Our interviews were very laid back and we often took on people who, in hindsight, weren't right, basically because we were so desperate for them – having 100 extra sets of accounts and no extra staff to take the work on will do that to you. For a long time we were constantly trying to catch up, and were unable to make best use of the data and our new client relationships because there simply wasn't time. We changed from that model to recruiting ahead of our plans.

The biggest thing you need to recruit and keep the right staff is a consistent HR process. I was an entrepreneur, so I built the business like an entrepreneur would. By the seat of my pants. At the beginning I had huge benefits because my business partner worked in the practice and set up files and processes to support my big-idea approach. But then she went, and it was just me. As I've said before, I'm not your typical accountant. I have a great team of good accountants, and I'm passionate about giving great service and being seen to be radical and informative, but I know I am less focused on conventional business processes, so some of these things got slightly lost.

James Kay on the right staff at the right time

I'm not a millennial and personally I don't go in for Wills big 'millennial' thing. I understand why he suggests it – it's good shorthand, and the people we hire generally tend to fit the millennial mould – but I think it's more about the qualities people have than what age they are. I'm not a millennial and I think I fit it quite well. So for me, recruitment of millennials is more about approach than when they were born.

> **Culture goes beyond personalities and is about work ethos**

Culture goes beyond personalities and is about work ethos. We want people we can rely on and who have a similar attitude to work as we do. That is where it becomes difficult. For us – for Will, Frances and me – it's our business. That said, generally I look for people who care.

The recruitment process

We don't really do interviews. We do chats. And we really don't have a formal interview process. There are no forms or tests. I've always said you can teach people skills, but you can't teach them their personality. If they're a fit personality-wise, you get that vibe about whether they're willing to learn. Then whether they can currently do a certain task is irrelevant. We may ask a few questions, but we're less interested in the technical side as we can see that on their CV. I want to make sure they fit with our people and our ideals of what we want our people to be.

Our chat is quite an experience for some people. They often look bewildered. They are looking for the usual questions, to be asked what their biggest challenge is and things like that.

> **Over time we've managed to identify what we really need, and now we're even more strict on the cultural fit**

Filling the skills gap

'We were so intent on getting bums on seats, we originally made the mistake of hiring on technical aptitude rather than culture. This wasn't a one-off, it happened over time. Now we know how hard it is to find the right people, so we work at it.' **Paul Bulpitt, The WOW Company**

What are millennials?

Although it's impossible to clearly define a group of around 80 million unique individuals, 'millennials' is the name given to a broadly defined group of people comprised of some Generation Y (born 1981-91) and Generation Z (born 1990-2001). Both grew up on computers and adapt easily. Generation Y grew up on PCs, mobile phones and video games while Generation Z has grown up on tablets, smartphones and apps. The common ground between them is: they tend to have different priorities and aspirations to those born before 1981; they were brought up at a time of more liberal politics and economics; they've been transforming and altering basic ideas about communication, aspiration and identity; and they believe they are the last generation able to save the planet.

'Before James was around, I struggled a bit with how to define the right people. We wanted people who fitted our culture, who can easily talk to clients, and to provide that laid-back image we want to promote. That's difficult to find. To start with, I relied heavily on other people to tell me if people were right in technical ways. This didn't always work. Over time we've managed to identify what we really need, and now we're even more strict on the cultural fit. We'd rather have someone who has the right approach who can learn than someone with all the right qualifications. We have the radio on, people chat, but people all work hard and things get done. That needs a certain sort of person.' **Frances Kay**

'Initially, when Will and Frances were recruiting before I started, they were so busy that they waited until the last possible second before hiring. That's why some of the people weren't a great fit. Will and Frances were desperate. Now we look ahead instead.' **James Kay**

'Earlier, we had people in the wrong roles. They had the right skills, but now if someone is good at one thing and less good at something else we try to help them do more of what they are good at, and find someone to backfill the other thing. It's much more beneficial for people to work 100% on what they are good at, and it's beneficial for us too.' **Frances Kay**

Performance appraisals, competency frameworks, pay bandings... Get your process right from day one

James Kay on setting it right: the MD's perspective

When I joined the firm, the three of us sat down and allocated roles and responsibilities on a spreadsheet so we didn't step on each other's toes. It took a while for Will to step away from some things, but neither he nor Frances are good at HR issues, while I am. For example, while they'd started working on pay structures and changing the way we deal with people to encourage staff retention, they hadn't necessarily executed all of it. Knowing what I'd done in the past, they were confident I'd be able to take that over very quickly.

Performance appraisals, competency frameworks, pay bandings… Get your process right from day one. Our biggest challenges have arisen because the HR, hiring and staff development process wasn't planned or wasn't clear to people.

I didn't know the industry. I still don't know it in the way Will and Frances do. I treat it the same as I would any business. You need a flow of work and people skilled to do that work. So my first priority was to understand what we do, learn the business and learn how the people fit around it. I had lots of interviews with staff, meeting everyone, talking to them, getting their thoughts and feelings. It was very interesting.

I believe you should never recruit the wrong person. I'd rather wait for the right person than cause myself a problem down the line

I discovered that people were frustrated with what they were doing. They were grouped into teams and the attitude was: 'This is my team and I won't do anything for anyone else because we have so much to do.' The skill point at junior levels of the company was very low, and people had been recruited as bums on seats rather than because they were right for the job. Unskilled or inappropriate people had been hired, and even those who had the right skills were often so beleaguered they felt they were making things worse. With everyone's backs against the wall with the workload, it's hard to find time to train junior members, and that made it worse. There was no succession planning and if anyone left suddenly it resulted in negativity, frustration and inevitable conflict between people.

Everyone knows they're on a similar wage, with a fixed framework from a starting or base level, and they can see how the wages increase as they work their way up

We couldn't afford to get more people, couldn't add more people – especially because I hadn't sorted the fee situation – and because of the company growth there was no cash to do it. I had to set my own expectations to manage this from the start.

I set out with a consistent message: that we don't do things half-heartedly, that we do things properly, we do things well and that the expectation of quality is

The Kays at work

'James and I are married. People told us we shouldn't work together, but why wouldn't I want to spend more time with my best friend? There have been no problems, and often we'll work late together or both work on a problem until it's sorted in a way that we couldn't if we weren't together.' **Frances Kay**

'We knew it wouldn't be an issue, both Will and Frances knew I was there to sort out some of the problems and issues they had no time or appetite for. It's come out quite well.' **James Kay**

firm-wide and a matter of pride. Once a structure had been established we very quickly saw which staff members wanted to come on our journey and those who were just collecting their wages. By tackling this and talking to them, they either became fed up or started thinking about what they did in a more positive way. Pretty much all the staff who weren't really a fit left after I instituted these discussions. Tackling the issues with the people concerned was all it took.

I remember one Friday I asked a particular guy if working as an accountant was really what he wanted. After the weekend he came to see me and told me he'd thought it over, it wasn't what he wanted and handed in his notice.

I believe you should never recruit the wrong person. I'd rather wait for the right person than cause myself a problem down the line. Even when we have vacancies I won't fill them – even at the highest level – until the right person presents themselves.

> **I don't want to pay recruitment fees for managers. That's ridiculous. We are growing our own future managers and we're deliberately overstaffing**

James Kay on transition planning

Yes, of course you might have a few gaps, but you can usually find a structure that works based on the people you have. As I said to Will and Frances, it costs a bit, but not too much if everyone works at 100%. Instead of firefighting (or at least feeling as if we are firefighting) we're thinking about who's going to do the work we need to do this year and next year. It's important to plan for the future, so if we get £100,000 of work tomorrow we could actually manage it. Yes, we'd need to create a couple more roles and add a new team, but we'd manage. We've got into the habit of planning for our growth, and in some respects are recruiting ahead of it rather than getting the work and then panicking.

I don't want to pay recruitment fees for managers. That's ridiculous. We're growing our own future managers and we're deliberately overstaffing in view of the work that's coming up. In some respects we also develop roles for people who are progressing well to allow them to have more responsibility as they grow. We can probably add 10% growth without recruiting any new roles, which I'd bet isn't normal. But it's much easier to bring a client into a functioning team than not.

Earlier we had a very different approach. Candidates would lead on what they wanted to study. Now we have rules. Young trainees start on AAT, or if they're going on the tax route, we look at tax-relevant options. We still want people who want to learn and want to better themselves.

The Tax and Pounds

Our pub-themed meeting room, The Tax and Pounds, is an important and well-loved part of Farnell Clarke HQ. The idea for a pub came from one of our team members and the fabulous name came from one of our Facebook friends, Laura Johnson.

The Tax and Pounds is open every Friday from 4pm and it's a great place for staff to socialise, have a drink and chat about the week. And of course, it's always open to those clients who prefer to talk business over a game of pool or with a drink in their hand (soft or otherwise).

Frances Kay on Improving business: the co-director's perspective

After James had spoken to everyone it was clear we needed a structure that clearly defined people's roles. Badly defined roles had lead to a lot of frustration and conflict as people were unwittingly treading on each other's toes. The welcome team here were doing the first three months with a new client, then passing it on to the permanent team. But there was no structure in the transition process, so people weren't sure what clients had – and had not – been told.

We changed that, and had a welcome person within each team from day one. The client would have the same experience, but the team would manage the process. This removed the areas where people clashed. It took a while, but it was really just about setting clearly defined roles, and where there were touch points, making sure it was clear where one person's responsibility ended and another's began.

We now have an organisation chart that maps directly onto all processes and procedure. Everybody knows who they are and how to fit in our organisation, and we review it periodically, starting at the top and working all the way through.

We have also instituted a clear career progression, with seniors helping trainees and the managers doing more with our clients. We also brought in a competency framework. Now everyone knows they're on a similar wage, with a fixed framework from a starting or base level, and they can see how the wages increase as they work their way up by gaining qualifications or demonstrating competence in certain tasks. Everyone's now very clear where they fit, and we've created visuals to summarise it. So, from the start you already know what you need to learn or do to get your next raise.

Obviously we've included CPD, but instead of booking people on occasional external courses, we brought it in-house. CPD is far easier now you can do it online, through webinars and recorded seminars and things like that. Plus because we can fit it into each individual's schedule rather than the other way round, we've been able to extend it to more people.

CASE STUDY
Simon Edrich of AccountsCo on KPIs

We've got all these KPIs now, so we know how many hours it takes to do anything in the office – how much time an average set of accounts or confirmation statement takes, or how long a bookkeeping transaction takes. The visibility it gives us is phenomenal. We now know exactly which clients take the most time, so taking a view as to how to manage that is much easier.

Look forward

As much as 75% of the workforce will be millennials by 2025 (yes I know I go on about it, but it's important!) and we wanted to be sure we appealed to this generation – as both staff and clients. We want clients who want to work with us because we have an edge. And the way our office is fitted out and the fact that we have a pub gives us something nobody else has got.

A few months after we opened *'The Tax and Pounds'* – our pub-themed meeting room – we saw a marked change in the attitude of people in the office. When you enjoy working somewhere, you're more productive, and that comes across to the client. People are supporting each other more cheerfully too.

Ways to make your office environment more attractive to potential staff and clients

- Get accreditation as a good employer to show new staff that existing staff enjoy their work.
  Not one of ours, but Sarah Wynne of Wynne and Co did this and it seems to work.

- Do cool stuff.
  We do!

- Give your clients cool stuff.
  We've had a good number of enquiries because people see our existing clients using Receipt Bank and they're intrigued. We give everyone Receipt Bank as part of our fixed-fee service.

- Show you're cool.
  Our office 'pub', The Tax and Pounds, is a cool meeting space with free wifi and a pool table available for anyone who would like to drop in and chat.

And finally

The right staff at the right time make for a successful firm, and our growth is in no small part a result of this. We've learned from our mistakes. Some have been costly, some not, but they've all given us valuable opportunities to rethink what we're doing and how we do it.

Chapter 5

Migrating to a fully digital cloud practice

· ·

Once a firm decides to become fully digital and has set its strategy, HR and operational support, there are also more pragmatic challenges to face. Since these days every accountancy firm has some kind of digital assistance or facilitation, what these challenges are will depend on the level of digital automation and supporting processes that already exist.

Foundation considerations to ensure a successful migration to a fully digital practice

- Ask yourself what your firm will look like in 12 months/three years. How much of a digital practice do you want to be? Are there easy ways for you to monitor and measure progress?

- Where are you now? If you're using some cloud products, you're already partially along the conversion process. Most people use the cloud to some extent these days, whether it's shared document drives, cloud-based servers or a suite of cloud-based apps. Understanding the extent to which staff and clients are doing so will help with getting buy-in, planning the tech change and understanding your priorities. Look at what has been tried so far and where the pain points are likely to be.

- Where are the gaps in skills, technology and process flow? Understanding tech, new processes, roles and responsibilities are key to a successful, frictionless implementation. After all, it's difficult to know how to proceed until you know where you are.

- Define what you want to deliver and when, and what you want to achieve from those deliveries.

- Are communication plans in progress? The client needs to be on board, to understand the benefits and trust that the change *will* benefit them – but so does management, and so do your staff.

- Is the management and staff buy-in sufficient? If not, how can that be changed?

But there's more

We didn't need – in the purest sense of the word – to do 90% of what we did to create a totally digital practice, and if you have strong reasons not to become fully digital then that is your strategic choice. I think there's one consistent thing that's true for all firms, irrespective of client base or their products and services – the more fully digital your firm becomes, the more value you will ultimately gain.

This Chapter

Migrating a firm's data and processes is not simple, but the potential gains are huge. This Chapter outlines our experiences of becoming a fully digital firm, has a great case study from a mid-tier firm who transferred their client data spectacularly well, and identifies some of the pitfalls.

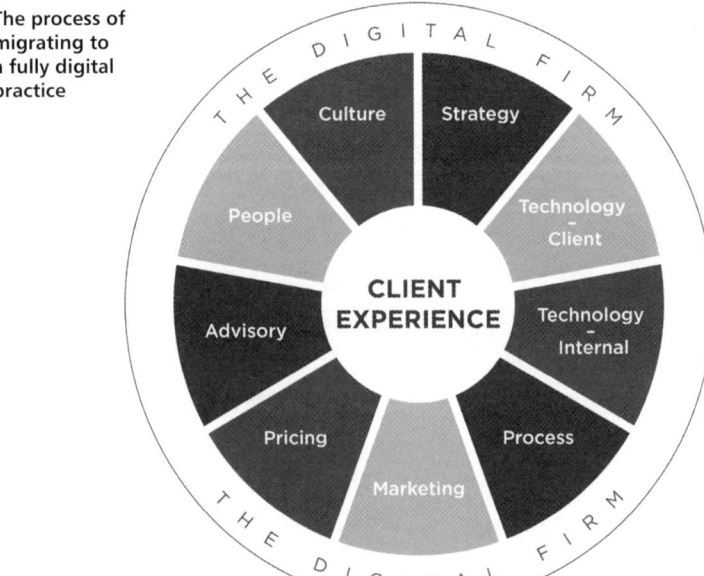

The process of migrating to a fully digital practice

Watch your language

Grant Smith of Armstrong Watson has his own take on the language used by firms: 'Some accountants who are only just adopting are using the 'cloud' as a pioneering term. Unfortunately it's not. I also get frustrated with competitors who perennially talk about the cloud because I kind of feel it was big five years ago. Think how long you've been able to store your personal photographs or documents online and you'll get an idea of how all-pervasive it already is. There might be a lot of late adopters who aren't yet using the cloud at all, but with the advent of MTD the government are putting a marker in the ground to say where compliance is going. You might be able to put your head in the sand right now, but you can't do that forever. The cloud's not a novelty any more – it's just where we do business.'

Indeed, full digital automation of work using the cloud is well established in other sectors, even though it's not yet the case with compliance and accountancy processes in general. As early adopters, Farnell Clarke wouldn't fall into the trap, but I can imagine a situation in which clients and potential clients might be taken aback or even alienated if the word was used to imply something new and revolutionary.

> **You might be able to put your head in the sand right now, but you can't do that forever**

Transitioning clients

Because we've always been as fully digital as it was possible to be, we hadn't experienced a large data migration in the way that other firms might. Whilst we had to tell people we were going to be using a cloud product, it wasn't quite the same. We were never in a position where we had to tell the client to do something completely different.

But in 2015 we moved 500 clients – from one cloud product to another. What makes this interesting is that nobody seems to have done this before. While migration of data from desktop tech was an established path

> **There were no existing processes for data migration between two cloud products, so we built our own software to make it possible**

facilitated by the app companies, there were no such existing facilitative processes for data migration between two cloud products, so we had to build our own software. It was a cost, and we decided to take on the cost of moving more data than Xero recommended because we felt it was the right thing to do. We had done our own migration of the rest inside 18 months, having built our own software to facilitate that migration.

Our migration process proved it wasn't as difficult as it might be. Like most firms, our clients trust us as advisors, so if we tell 50 clients there's a better option on the market, they accept our expertise. Even though firms see this change as a barrier, and that migration to the cloud creates challenges, when we get into the midst of doing the conversion we find that these challenges aren't as significant as we might first think.

Making the move

Most people will be moving from the desktop, which means that Xero (or the cloud provider of your choice) will cover the cost of moving two years of data.

In 2015, when we moved clients from KashFlow to Xero, that was a significant change. Back then nobody had built a cloud to cloud migration product – the whole idea of cloud accounting was still very new. Cloud to cloud is now an option through all usual suppliers.

> There's often a feeling that you should give someone the role of tech champion, appoint someone to champion the tech to the clients, but buy-in needs to happen through the whole firm. Some of the leading firms need a huge amount of time to transition, but that presents an opportunity for some of the smaller firms. The fast movers will take on the mantle.
>
> **Matt Flanaghan, BlueHub**

There were lots of options for moving on. For example, clients could move two years of desktop data to Xero, and since Xero normally does that for free, from the clients' point of view they're getting extra-fast reports.

The move was a big challenge for us. For a long time, when I talked about becoming a digital practice and using digital technology, we hadn't had to move legacy clients.

While we migrated data between cloud platforms, Armstrong Watson migrated the data of 4,500 clients from desktop and manual apps in just 18 months. That's phenomenal. The sheer number of clients they migrated was out of this world. That is why we've used them as a case study below.

CASE STUDY

Grant Smith on Armstrong Watson's huge migration

Armstrong Watson is a 10-office mid-tier firm that employs about 400 people. Back in 2010 one of my clients was an Apple Mac fan, and for some reason Sage didn't want their software on Apples. Xero had been around for about a year, so my client signed up with them, rang me up and asked me what I thought. I'd never heard of them, so got them to do me a sales demo. Once I saw their bank reconciliation feature, I was sold.

At that point, Sage was the market leader, but by the time the clients had handed over the backup, you'd find the bank wasn't balanced. In many cases that pretty much meant we'd have to start from scratch for each client. Although Xero still needed a fair degree of improvement, the system encouraged the client to reconcile the bank accounts. Towards the end of the year, Xero had improved to the point I was sure we should be using it, and I embarked on the long and painful journey of trying to encourage a mid-tier firm to migrate client data to the cloud.

The first step was establishing a partnership with Xero. The idea of a partnership didn't mean anything for Xero, but for our firm it was a really big thing, so even after a couple of clients had signed up themselves it took six months. The next year was spent working out who was the best partner to go with. We had lots of 'beauty parades'– including ones with FreeAgent, QuickBooks and Sage One – until I experienced what in my blog I called my 'Brian Clough moment' and the partners finally agreed with what I said.

Xero partners are given rewards according to the number of clients they migrate to the system, each of which brings different partner status and rewards. Armstrong Watson achieved platinum status inside 18 months. Over that time we went through bronze and silver into gold, and while conversions to Xero included a smattering of clients around the firm, most were mine. In 2016, we embarked on a bit of a drive, acquiring a group of organisations already on Xero and by doing that we became platinum. Migrating 500 businesses onto Xero when we had around 5,000 potential businesses was one of my more hollow moments, because we weren't achieving our potential.

> **I decided that, rather than taking colleagues to XeroCon, I'd take the influencers**

At the same moment as the firm moved from office reporting to service-line reporting I decided that, rather than taking colleagues to Xerocon, I'd take the influencers. A conference of around 1,300 accountants in one room generates a buzz. I managed to get our CEO Paul Dixon some face time with Xero's CEO, Rod Drury. Both Paul and Toby Woodhead (Armstrong Watson's solutions architect who deals with internal projects) both got it, and also visited the 50 or 60 add-on partners at the conference. After that we discussed what we'd learned as a firm, what we'd already achieved and what we could do. Because I'd been involved for so long, I had my vision and tried to persuade them to it. We decided to go for it. I wanted our accounts production on Xero (we were unique in that). I persuaded the service-line head and worked on the strategy of converting 4,500 clients from old accounting software to Xero. That doesn't mean we have 4,500 active clients using Xero, but it does mean we have their data on Xero.

Nowadays we use AutoEntry for clients to get data into Xero. We are a northern firm, and still have quite a lot of shoebox clients. We take bank statements, scan them on, and set up bank rules. The system basically reconciles your account for you. While there's an element of set-up time in the first year, we save much more time in the long run.

Internal process re-engineering

We've also taken the opportunity to have a 'back to the beginning' look at how we raise accounts. While Xero is the cornerstone, we are always looking for historic things to stop doing. For example, we now use variance reports for issues, and it has meant significant time savings.

Resources

It's in resourcing that most planning was required. We took it upon ourselves to do the data conversion from SAP to Xero, developed our own tool and in eight months had converted the data of 4,500 clients. There was an element of trial and error, but once our tool had been developed it took weeks rather than months.

What is a tech champion?

I think every firm needs a tech champion – not necessarily someone on the board, but someone in the business with plenty of non-chargeable time who can influence and persuade, to get everyone on board with the idea of forging ahead when it comes to tech. Ideally this person is both good at communicating and is a geek who'll want to go to the conferences, read the magazines, show clients how to use software and provide that bit of extra understanding about how tech will work and support clients.

Will Farnell, Farnell Clarke

Planning migration

It's important to consider what kind of questions we need to ask. I think the starting point is how much of your client base you want to migrate, and bear in mind the software that the client already has. Then look at your client base and decide who you really want to move and which clients you are happy to see leave. That gives you a number – let's say it's 300 clients. You then decide how many you're going to move per month. Matt Flanagan of BlueHub has a tool he uses to estimate the amount of time it will take different firms to migrate to the cloud. Given the clients and the transfer rate, he can provide the completion date with a remarkable level of accuracy.

> **Once you decide to migrate fully to the cloud, you need to commit the resources**

Understanding how quickly you can migrate client data is important, but so is the driver. Is it MTD, the opportunity that data transfer will provide for building better client relationships, better value-added services or firm-wide efficiency? It should be all of them of course, but many firms still don't see it this way.

To start with, Farnell Clarke just tinkered around the edges of the migration, and it didn't get us anywhere. Once we put the right level of resource on it, the conversion and migration just happened. And that's the important thing to remember – once you decide to migrate fully to the cloud you need to commit the resources.

> **Variance reports for issues have meant significant time savings**

Perspective in numbers

We were innovators on the early-adopter curve and we often weren't able to find tech to fulfil particular business needs. My view is we're still in early adoption. Numbers from the software companies indicate there are about 400,000 users of cloud accounting software. However there are 4.5 million small businesses in the UK, so the take-up is still pretty small.

What I mean is that Receipt Bank, QuickBooks, Xero and KashFlow have just 10% of the accounting market. Of course there are other products out there, but it's an indicator that anyone moving to total cloud accounting is an early adopter – even now.

There are still people out there who have no idea what all this stuff is about. You have conversations with them and see how concerned they are. When we hear everything they have is on desktop we ask how they are going to deal with MTD. One potential staff member's answer was that he was here for an interview so wouldn't have to deal with it. I'll leave you to imagine how we responded to that.

From add-on to ad-hoc development

While we work with the same basic suite of products, our clients often ask for advice about the additional apps that can be used. Because our customers are all different, the way we do this can vary, but here are some of Frances's experiences to show how we manage them.

'A new customer wants certain approval levels on purchases. The client needs multiple access levels – one level for the person who does the donkey work, one to approve it, another on expense reports and possibly more. Xero alone doesn't do that, so I did some research and booked myself onto demos of other software. I've not used these products and I don't know if they're any good, so I start with apps that are rated highly by customers or that I've seen at Xerocon. After I've compared them, I put the pros and cons into a small database so I have the details for next time, and so I can tailor my advice to the client to make sure I suggest the apps that best suit them.

'There are companies who have set themselves up to research and integrate, but we only do first-level integration research, then you learn with the client on the product. It's hard, and it's important to talk about what you find and what you think. I work hard to make sure any advice I give the client is well researched and fits their culture and approach. Then we use it and learn together. For example, on the expenses report, I looked at Expensify, webexpenses and, of course, Receipt Bank, which I always look at first because it's included in the package to the client.' **Frances Kay**

Staff training

One of the issues that many firms have is a chicken-and-egg staff training situation (whether firms should train before they need to or after). Firms shouldn't wait until they NEED the training. They should try to stay ahead of the game, so they can demonstrate competency to potential clients. For Farnell Clarke it was never an issue. We want clients and potential clients to visit the office and see confident, competent teams already working in a seamless, transparent way, and while it took a while to achieve that, the question was never about their training. Besides, the more staff using Xero every day, the more expertise we're developing, and the more easily we can give clients a service to our high standards. Also the confidence and competence of the staff shows when they network.

You learn with the client on the product

Unintended and unanticipated consequences

The biggest unintended consequence of committing to being a fully digital firm is that we recruited a lot of younger people. We might, under other circumstances, have gone for quality and experience over personalities, but we're very particular now. We need our potential employees to have the right attitude before anything else, and for them to be into computing and tech.

The sole practitioner

Considering a sole practitioner as opposed to small, medium and large firms shows that it's all relative. A sole trader will be working with fewer clients. Their challenge is in the resourcing. A sole practitioner might have as many as 100 clients, and that means at least two conversations a week as well as their day job, just to get to the point where they can talk to their clients about why they might change and the processes involved. This type of firm might well feel the need to get someone in to support the process, while a 10-staff firm will have more clients but probably more resources as well. It's not that they will have free resources – I don't know any accountants that aren't really busy, regardless of client numbers – but larger firms are more likely to have the opportunity to dedicate an internal resource to conversion, while sole traders won't.

Continuous improvement

Between a year and 18 months after the data was migrated and staff and clients were trained, we embarked on the first regular periodic review of how we do business and who does what. Frances's words summarise this well: 'The first focus was to get the structure right in terms of teams – people playing to their strengths instead of square pegs in round holes. Then it was time to start using them to develop and refine the processes for us. We started with a couple of people, looking at how they do stuff, how it's documented and what might be improved.'

Make it compulsory?

If you've decided to go through a dramatic change, such as a firm-wide migration of client data to Xero, you need to convert the clients too and should consider making it compulsory. If you leave anybody with options, they're likely to choose the option of least resistance. If this happens, the firm will lose much of the benefit.

Things we did wrong: tips, tricks and bootstraps

We've done lots of things wrong. Because we were too early to market, we didn't have the choice that now exists. When we took on KashFlow it was a great product, but over time Xero's pace of development was faster. However, we were lucky. I think it comes back to having clients and staff with a millennial attitude – we had clients prepared to take the risk with us. Our clients are also innovators who want to be a part of new developments. They wanted to use new stuff, and would accept that sometimes, because it was leading-edge, it wouldn't work as it should.

Our rapid growth meant we moved offices four times in seven or eight years. I think the difficulty came because I wasn't aware of how quickly we could grow the business. The overall message of this is good, though. If you get your offer right, your firm will benefit considerably. Very few firms have had our growth profile over these years.

Benefits of data management in the fully digital firm

- A simplified compliance process, because so much is automated.
- Insights into performance, growth and opportunities for both firm and clients.
- Rapid analysis of risky projects or ventures providing early warnings for the most probable pitfalls.
- Automated management accounts.
- Repeatable transparent systems.
- Transfer of responsibility to comply with regulatory changes in tech requirements.

And finally

No amount of digitisation is worthwhile if we lose sight of our objectives. For Farnell Clarke that means keeping clients out of jail (compliance, of course) and providing them with a leading edge excellent service.

Chapter 6

The inextricable link

. . . .

A t Farnell Clarke we're constantly looking for ways to use tech to free up staff time and develop more regular communications with clients to better understand our clients needs and provide better value-added services. While the degree to which you choose to contact clients and the methods you use to communicate internally with staff may change according to your firms strategy, every digital firm will find their services, products, marketing, sales and internal and external communications inextricably linked. Effective use and documentation of those communications therefore becomes a critical success factor in the development of a successful digital firm.

Points to consider in your digital firm's communication strategy:

- Incorporate all methods of communication into an easily managed workflow.
- Keep up! Let young staff and clients brief you on potential new trends in social media and communications. Being aware of new methods of communication doesn't mean you have to adopt them, but if your target clients have established a pattern it's worth considering adopting their communications mode to provide services on their levels.
- Be consistent. If you're providing 24/7 responses (even if the out of hours responses only come in the form of an acknowledgement), then such acknowledgements should be consistently given. This means you need to understand and document the clients' preferences as part of business as usual.

- Record everything automatically. This is a big ask, but if you don't, client concerns might get lost overnight, say if a staff member acknowledges the client's concern late one evening and then forgets to act on it the next day.

But there's more

For us, effective communication isn't necessarily easy or fast. It might be faster to send an email to a client rather than picking up the phone, and it might feel easier at the time, but we need to interact with our clients in different and sometimes more personal ways. It's not possible to understand their concerns – their niggles and what keeps them up at night – or provide good-value services unless we interact with them well (as opposed to writing one-way emails or old-fashioned letters). Also, working with our clients' preferred communications modes brings additional challenges in managing the wide range of communications protocols chosen by our clients, and is why we're developing our own CRM system.

This Chapter

This chapter, important despite its relative brevity, discusses challenges in the development of communications, and in particular how communications has become the glue that holds everything together.

Controlling the data is half the challenge, and communicating with the client is the other half

Solving the biggest issue

The biggest problem we have to stop is this 'once a year' mentality, shared by clients and accountants alike. And we can. Easily available data, all year round, has huge potential benefits and can give firms and clients much more. I've said it before, but take it another step and automate the client's bookkeeping for them and you're no longer dependent on the client completing their data entry (and associated accuracy challenges) plus you get the benefits of planning your workflow better. Take it one step further, and you can be working with and communicating with the client all year round. Such regular communication enables you to look for other services to deliver as well as how to deliver them more efficiently. Controlling the data is half the challenge, and communicating with the client is the other half.

Communication = training = business development

Frances Kay from Farnell Clarke says, 'Regular communication is as much about training the clients in new ways of thinking as it is learning more about them and keeping a running dialogue – and it starts from the very first meeting. For example, we saw a potential new client recently. They have an incredibly manual process for sales invoices. We suggested they get their developers to integrate directly with Xero. That will take a significant chunk off our quoted bill, and they said they definitely would. We did ourselves out of work but equally we're in for the long haul and I doubt anyone here would have enjoyed managing the process anyway.'

CRM

Our own CRM system eliminates the need for copying documents, ticking boxes and making sure that disparate types of client communication aren't lost. We want the client to be able to see it, so if they ask for something that isn't already being done they will see everything, from the initial change request – which they will raise – to when it reaches the account manager, and whether there are charges or responses needed.

Keeping client confidence = fast responses

Frances Kay says, 'It makes me antsy if I have an inbox of emails that haven't been replied to. I want to build our clients' trust, help them when they need it and understand how we can add value to our services to them in the future. When I joined Farnell Clarke, the account manager was new and because all she was doing was concentrating on meeting deadlines, the whole client relationship had suffered. In fact those who weren't accustomed to just calling barely knew who their client manager was! Now everyone replies quickly, our policy is to respond to clients within 24 hours, even during weekends and even if that response is just a holding email.'

Fast responses must be backed by actions

Frances says, 'Because we know that a fast response is important to our clients who need to be able to share their concerns, we do our best to respond 24/7 – even if it's just to acknowledge receipt of their communication. I have a client who WhatsApps me or calls me late into the weekend. He'll email first but if he doesn't get an immediate response he'll try other ways to get me to respond. That's fine, but I have to ping myself to make sure I remember to follow up the communication when the new week starts.'

'When you read and respond to a message but are doing something else, it's easy for what you've discussed or acknowledged to slip your mind. With the best will in the world, unless an action based on that communication is not on the job flow for the next day, I'll forget about it. Of course, if a message arrives on an individual's work number as opposed to the Farnell Clarke WhatsApp account, which is automatic. That's a challenge we expect to fix with a new app we're developing in-house.'

James Kay on the inextricable link

Although we are constantly working on the link between communication, marketing, sales and operations, it's still an area we could certainly make more use of. It's not rocket science – it's just the way it is and I'm on board with it.

If anything, the biggest struggle we have is in time management. We really need to make the most of our communications with clients and be clear that the right way to interact with them is not necessarily the easiest way. When time is limited, the easiest thing to do is send an email. Using lots of different ways to communicate, market and link things up is great when you have loads of time to do it, and I see these new one-man-band start-ups do it really well. We have more than 1,000 clients to factor in. We're working on improving our communications and it will come with time. Giving staff and clients alike a consistent message, then doing it, is how we're getting there.

CASE STUDY
Will Farnell on Farnell Clarke

We are a practice that utilises a mix of digital tech and digitally aware staff to deliver first class services effectively and efficiently to maximum levels of automation. That's effectively our strategy. We have to differentiate our offering, which for us includes digital marketing, digitally savvy people and a consistent internal and external approach. That is our sales strategy.

Frances Kay on using good communication to develop business

In one conversation, one of our clients wondered about expense-reporting apps that managed VAT claims. It wasn't part of my actual role, but we did demos on lots of reporting tools that sync with Xero so that we could go back to the client, talk about what each product does, and go through the ups and downs of each. As we develop an increasing in-house knowledge of these apps, we can keep an eye out for what other clients might need, asking them why they don't have a certain app, or what they're doing to automate a particular function of their business.

Mileage is another of those weird things worth bringing up in conversation. Tripcatcher is less than £5.00 per month, and if used would automatically end up in the data every month.

CASE STUDY
Grant Smith of Armstrong Watson
on staff communications

With the data for more than 4,500 clients on board we launched the new Armstrong Watson way, an approach that spans internal communications and external clients. Part of that was providing three days of training for 200 people. This wasn't just about Xero, but how we want to do business, how our apps and systems work together and more. It was quite a challenge.

I've always said to my staff that if we don't change we'll die – now we're living it. We have continuous briefings. Richard Andrew, our service-line head, does a weekly team video. It's only five minutes and it's great. People don't have to wait around for the availability of a physical training session and everyone's learning a little every week.

And finally

'We now have the tax team, the business team and the onboarding process. Now we want to nail the communications and the CRM we've been developing to make our lives easier. The beauty of our set-up is that both Will and Frances are having conversations with loads of people – potential clients, app partners and more. We have loads of opportunity and no reason to expect our year-on-year growth will slow down for a while. While the other two are developing business, I'm all about nailing the core service first and then working on improvements. So far it's going well.' **James Kay**

Chapter 7

Putting forward perspectives

···

Marketing is a wasted activity unless it is closely linked to what you are trying to achieve. This means you need to have an overarching strategy in terms of making your firm different. When you understand what differentiates you, you need to be able to shout it from the rooftops. Lots of firms I talk to do some really great stuff (for example they might have huge experience in a particular sector and, knowing its pain points, be in a position to help others). The important thing is to understand what you want to be known for as a firm, and making it consistent with the way you present your firm externally.

That's why marketing is key. It's no longer merely about getting new clients in this fast-paced interconnected world – it's about maintaining a presence, establishing your desirability with partners or even potential mergers and acquisitions (depending on your exit strategy). It's also about establishing your desirability for staff, which you've seen in Chapter 6, *If you build it they will come*, but it's worth repeating that as more millennials join the jobs market – and become potential clients – this will become increasingly important.

Five ways to help clients find their way to your firm.

- **Prioritise your coverage**
  To find a good spread of clients, it's first important to be very clear about who they are, where they go and what they look at. From that, prioritise your time and energy and plan accordingly.

- **Update your website**
  According to Adobe, 38% of people will stop engaging with a website if the content or layout is unattractive. When redesigning, don't forget that these days mobile devices account for two thirds of all time spent online.

- **Use social media effectively**
  It's a place to build relationships, establish a niche, maintain profile and more. I'll look at this more in the next chapter, but this is a marker that content marketing is the most important part of social media marketing, and it needs to be embedded into strategy.

- **Maximise email marketing efforts**
  While most firms communicate with clients regularly via email, most still aren't fully exploiting the opportunity. Make your content eye-catching and your ideas attractive.

- **Keep blogging**
  Blogs showcase a firm's knowledge and insight, provide regular content to support social media campaigns, and can even help push a site up search-engine rankings. But to be effective it needs to be consistent.

But there's more

Keep a sense of proportion. Nobody has unlimited resources, whether that's staff, time or money. As I said above, prioritisation is vital. It's hard to remember at times, but it's important to not feel we should do everything at once – or even ever. I've found it vital to stay clear about who our clients and potential clients are, who we want them to be, their preferred communications methods and their concerns. Focusing on that brings results.

This Chapter

Developing an internal appreciation of the fully digital practice requires a change in approach. This is as true for those who are initiating the change at the highest level as it is all the way down to each staff member and also for our clients and this is what we'll examine here.

Setting the Scene

A Xero partner benchmarking study demonstrates that raising questions regarding a firm's position in the market helps practices agree and articulate their strategy for up to six years. Much of this strategy should be around identifying and attracting clients, but Xero's findings indicate that much of the industry still isn't investing in marketing to the extent I think they should.

Marketing is therefore vital. Face to face will always be key, but maintaining a meaningful online profile has increasing importance: firstly, because even referred

Five important marketing pointers for the digital firm

1. Trust is paramount,

2. Build awareness before attracting potential clients,

3. Let the client come to you when they're ready,

4. ROI is the end game, but it goes beyond financial return,

5. Measure ROO as well as ROI,

6. Keep your marketing plan simple

clients like to check up on a firm before approaching them; and secondly, because an increasingly mobile market will be relying on what they find online rather than the people they meet. So while networking in conferences demonstrates our value – and sells us – to communities of interest and the old gang, our target market of millennials need to see a credible dynamic online presence as part of their decision-making process.

As you can see, when it comes to the big picture of marketing for the digital practice, it's as much about changing our mindsets – thinking more like business owners and less like accountants – as it is actually setting out marketing plans.

Karen Reyburn's viewpoint is particularly relevant here: 'The very traits that make you a wonderful accountant actually betray you when it comes to marketing. They make you a perfectionist, help you prevent penalties. They are detailed and make you ruthless. With accounting there's a 'right' and a 'wrong'. There are rules, and you have to follow the rules to get your accounts right. When it comes to marketing these very same habits will destroy you because that's not how marketing works.'

> **The very traits that make you a wonderful accountant actually betray you when it comes to marketing**

Karen goes on to explain her experience. Accountants are great at what they do, and many know it, they have decades of experience. They come to marketing with all this experience and great business knowledge and they ask for an answer – they ask for a specific, definable thing, where the thing is an action, a product or a behaviour. They ask if they should do social media or write a blog. They ask about whether they should have a website. They want particular, easily definable answers, but it's not that easy. Maybe one successful firm has no website at all, and another would never get leads if it wasn't for their website.

In marketing, rules don't apply. Anything goes, and it's important to look at things from a different point of view to develop a marketing plan that works. Karen encourages her clients first to acknowledge that marketing requires this different approach, and that going with a regular accountant's approach is likely to fail. Marketing is human and messy, and making mistakes is a good thing because they help you learn. It's is about building relationships, taking time and not getting instant results. That's a big and important change to take on. Karen explains that none of the normal expectations are right, and that she can advise firms of approaches, but it's important to follow a pattern and not specific rules.

Karen Reyburn of The Profitable Firm on core elements

There are a breadth of possibilities for how you might consider your marketing plan. I'd say that the core elements I'd encourage any accountant to address is their brand, their website and their communications – these are how you engage with clients and prospects. Then it depends. The first thing you might communicate might be about your new service or approach, or internal changes that reflect added value for your clients. Some firms need a major rebrand, with a new firm name and a new logo, a video or other visual method to reflect the changes they have already made. If they're a big firm with 80 staff or more, they need to show off these changes. For smaller firms with fewer team members, it's perfectly fine to have a simple logo and build their own websites.

'One firm with multiple partners and owners all over the world shares blog posts on LinkedIn because that's the best way for them to make sure their message reaches different locations. Another firm does everything on Facebook and Instagram because that's where the companies they work with – online retail companies – hang out. This might make it sound like changes in marketing are dependent on size. They're not, but there are different ways to address brands and communications. Once you have the core elements, it comes down to who your audience is. This shouldn't be about you, but more about your organisation. You're the accountant and you need to build something that appeals to your target audience. Your marketing and website – and anything else – needs to match your target audience.

Niche or not?

You're either the cheapest or you're demonstrably different. Firms out there are doing compliance from £20 a month, so unless you want to go in that direction your only other option is to differentiate your offering. Accountants are good at saying they're different – you'll see that on all of their websites – but actually they're the same. It's important to become proactive, to demonstrate

Once you've identified your difference, promote it

a depth of experience and, once you've identified your difference, promote it. Accountants aren't often good marketeers and are reluctant to hire someone in, but marketing will become ever more important as mobile millennials look unceasingly for the firm that suits their businesses and their approach.

Market Positioning

We were providing a service that nobody else using this technology had produced, and it became a key part of our growth. At the point of publishing this book, there's still a great opportunity since take-up's still pretty low. In certain regions of the UK there are only one or two firms who get it – some are way ahead, but there's a big gap between those front-runners and the rest of the pack. It's at this point the whole idea of tech stops becoming a differentiator and what you do with it starts becoming key.

It's at this stage you might think about niche markets, and if that doesn't fit you well, you'll need to think about what else gives you that differentiation. If you're a traditional firm and your past USP has been that you are a full-service firm, or a mid-tier firm with access to lots of additional service lines, then consider how you might incorporate things. In doing this you'll find out how to get the value of the cloud, and use your current market positioning to boost that.

> **We have found that clients generally don't want to feel there is a lighter touch**

A lot of firms have gone wrong by trying to create a cheaper sub-brand within their accounting business. With cloud accounting this causes confusion and provides conflicting messages. The client is likely to think that since they are being forced into taking a new, cheaper product, they are no longer getting what the firm has stood for. It's difficult to demonstrate value in such cases. That's why new branding isn't what online accounting is about, irrespective of how it is perceived.

For a cheaper sub-brand to work we have to deliver something with a very light touch and – if absolutely necessary – demonstrate where it results in cheaper options. Actually, we've found that clients generally don't want to hear there's a lighter touch, and they definitely don't want to lose contact altogether – they still want the guidance of their accountants. Once you position online services as cheap it's difficult to deliver the value you should be providing. Instead of rebranding or offering cloud computing as a cheap options, rethink your core message and look at how you can use the tech along with the greater time flexibility the cloud enables for your core business.

CASE STUDY

Frances Kay on networking

It's nice to be able get out of Norwich more. That's about networking with the right people. Back near our head office I did a talk at Santander to local businesses on cloud accounting. We're also sponsoring the food and drink awards, because hospitality is a sector we're good at and are working on.

I'm also enthusiastic for our younger staff to go to networking events. They can sell on to their peers too, and it's nice for them to get out of the office. I've also joined a few other groups, such as one comprised of a group of high-flyer women. These events have a lot of value. We should all be doing more.

On other levels entirely, we're also distributing leaflets and setting up an event with guests who will address issues that a particular target sector has. These are learning experiences and we will see what comes from the results.

Reports by various experts talk about the interest and importance of marketing increasing as firms add online clients. They claim both interest and importance taper off slightly once firms have substantial experience, and that firms with robust online client portfolios shift their focus from the fundamentals of marketing and pricing of their services to more advanced marketing topics, like how to position their services. Whether this really happens remains to be seen, but it's important to be sure of our services, and our potential clients and where to find them, before we spend time and resources on focused business development.

And finally

The accountancy sector is changing dramatically – and it's changing fast. The most successful firms have embraced digital technology and its attendant marketing challenges are finding new and better ways to deliver excellent results and enhanced profitability. But we know from talking to other firms that some practices are finding both the idea of change, and the transition itself, more challenging than others. We've been setting new benchmarks in digital accountancy and innovation for more than 10 years and this means we've seen first-hand the wild challenges this new landscape present.

From using the cloud to streamline processes to developing new software to aid practice management, we've always been keen to challenge the status quo and find new ways to stand out from the crowd. All this has made our business more profitable and sustainable, and has helped us develop a loyal client base and a national reputation for innovation.

All this, though, depends on developing a resilient and pragmatic marketing strategy – one that enables us to learn, and that helps us understand existing and potential clients. It's this openness to new ways of doing things and pragmatism in prioritisation of the marketing and business development that's key to putting forward any firm's perspectives. The way these perspectives are expressed is key to attracting the type of clients we want to work with in the future.

Chapter 8

Content marketing for the digital firm

· ·

A s a financial professional, you have the skills to help businesses from inception and throughout their development. Getting small-business owners to recognise your value and hire you starts with an open mind, by putting yourself in their shoes and by letting go of many of the entrenched ideas of marketing you might not have questioned before.

These days service and marketing are inextricably linked. Marketing is no longer merely about interacting with current and potential clients, but also about establishing your desirability for potential new staff. I talk more about millennials, client communication and engagement in much of the rest of the book. This one is devoted to marketing planning.

Information hoarding is dead. Don't forget the old face-to-face methods. Having a great brand, going to high quality conferences, building a solid CRM, being clear on your pricing, running great events, and building a beautiful website – these are all still vital, and will be dealt with. But to make it all work – and to know where to prioritise – you need to focus on your target audience, and the new way of doing marketing, because it's all about your potential buyer.

Target audience, marketing, products, going online and creating efficiencies are part of your survival strategy. You'll see more about this throughout the book.

When developing your content-marketing plan...

- Measure ROO as well as ROI (for more on this see Chapter 8, *Content marketing for the digital firm*).
- Remember relationships are at the heart of marketing.
- Build awareness.
- Build trust over time.
- Let the client come to you when they're ready.
- Keep your marketing plan simple.

But there's more

Depending on the size and age of the firm or its current status it might not be possible – or desirable – to do everything we might want. That's fine, but it means we have to be creative, sure of our priorities and understand exactly what we're doing and why we're doing it. We need that anyway, but it becomes particularly important when we're working to a restricted budget or with limited time.

While the best-performing firms do all of this in-house, a pragmatic halfway step is to do a combination of contracted out-of-house and in-house work. This is why I invited Karen Reyburn of The Profitable Firm, a creative agency working exclusively with accountants, to contribute her structured approach and breadth of thinking to this chapter.

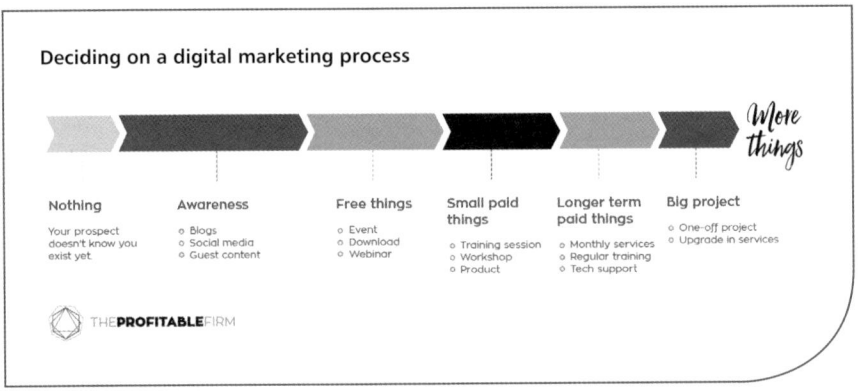

This Chapter

We'll examine how a productive, pragmatic content marketing strategy fits with other aspects of the digital firm throughout this book. Nothing should be considered in isolation. This chapter establishes a measurable rationale for creating and implementing a marketing plan with particular emphasis on content, and what that means, because we're all familiar with the more traditional aspects of marketing already.

Karen Reyburn on changing your mindset

Karen Reyburn says, 'These days, when we talk about 'marketing', what we really mean is 'content marketing'. The definition of content marketing is 'teaching and problem-solving to earn buyer trust'. At The Profitable Firm, we've been using content marketing for a long time: first because it's what every buyer wants, and second to show an example to the accountants we serve about how marketing is done.

Accountants who are marketing 'the old way' are looking primarily at your return on investment (ROI). You are evaluating each marketing action individually, and you're making marketing decisions based on what you can instantly see will have a direct impact.

This doesn't work anymore.

The old way of evaluating ROI on an element-by-element basis

> **The old way of evaluating ROI on an element-by-element basis is dead**

is dead. You can't even ask your prospects how they found you (was it your website? social media? email?), because all your marketing integrates together.

The new way is to start by determining ROO: Return on objective. This means considering what your particular purpose is in your marketing efforts. Are you building awareness? Getting specific, direct leads? Changing the perception of your brand? Differing objectives result in differing marketing efforts, and attempting to see ROI without addressing ROO will leave you frustrated and with very poor results.

The heart of content marketing

Accountants are amazing at building and keeping relationships. You know your clients well. You care about them.

Content marketing reflects the fact that this relational element must be brought into your marketing before the prospect becomes a client, so that they can build a foundational level of trust that will help them make their decision to work with you.

Think about all the important relationships you have now in life. Did you connect with them instantly? Or did much of the relationship build over time? For most relationships, there was a small connection that led to a greater one and now, many years on, you can't imagine life without that person in it.

Put all those feelings together and you get what we're looking to create in content marketing. This is the heart of trust-building, and when it's done with consistency, it will build that funnel you've been dreaming of, which will present a continual drip feed of quality new clients to you on a regular basis.

The point of all this marketing work is to build relationships with your prospects as well as with your clients. This may feel exhausting, or pointless ('what if they don't become a client and I've wasted all this time?'), but I assure you that without it, your new prospect is not going to last long as a client.

It's not only the firm owner who has to be part of this relationship building. Everyone in your firm can be a teacher to your clients and potential clients. When it comes to marketing, the highest performing accounting firms involve their entire team, because that's who your clients are going to be working with on a longer term basis. You need to begin the content marketing process the same way you intend to continue the client experience process.

Getting the team to buy in will take time. It will be hard, and take many small steps, to help those you hired to be accountants realise their role in the bigger marketing picture for the firm. It will also be the single best change you can make in your firm – not only for the sake of your potential clients, but also for the sake of your team members. You're building their connection, their investment, their enthusiasm for the firm – not simply for doing some work with numbers and going home.

Accountants are used to starting with the lowest-level marketing questions. 'What marketing action do I need to take? And what will I get from it?' Content marketing takes a great leap backwards and says, 'Why am I doing this at all? And who am I doing it for?'

You can still ask what marketing actions you'll take. But before you start thinking about whether you need to be using Facebook, if you have to start blogging, and whether you need a new website, stop all that and step back.

Go back to the person. The relationship. When you know who you want to work with, specifically, you're starting in the right place. Marketing is about them: their traits, their values, their industry, their business type. And your messaging then is about them, too. Their needs, confusions, issues.

Ask yourself what they actually want and need, and talk about those things. Answer their questions. Help them with their problems. Right their wrongs. Only once you've done that do you then ask what format your content will take (a blog post, a video, a website page).

Everyone in your firm can be a teacher

This approach can take longer than you expected, but it brings you the highest quality clients who have an extremely high-level of trust. Isn't that better than a high quantity of prospects who aren't sure yet, don't know if they need you, and end up leaving your firm for another?

When it comes to the issues and problems your clients face, I could easily give you a 400-point list of the questions that people ask of their accountants. But that's not the point.

Remember that marketing is not a formula that you follow, with clearly defined rules, and everything in black and white. It's not like accounting. It's grey. It changes all the time. It's different for each person and each firm. You need to build your own relationships with prospects, and the relationship you build will be different from anyone else's. You will experience a return on your prospect relationships, and as with all the best relationships, it will take time.

Because marketing doesn't have an easy formula with boxes to tick, you will not get it perfectly right the first time. Failure – the way accountants have historically thought about success or failure in marketing – is actually not a problem in content marketing, because it tells you something. What didn't work? How can you change it? And most importantly, are you still focusing on your ROO, or have you slipped back into trying to get ROI from one specific marketing medium?

It isn't simply about ROI. It's not about what your firm does and whether you're doing it in the right format. It's not enough to say, 'Well, I've shared videos on YouTube for a month and it didn't work for me because it didn't generate any new clients.' Your conclusions are premature. Remember that the reason you're doing this is to build trust with potential buyers. Keep doing what you're doing to build engagement. Interest. Questions. Noticeability.

> **The importance of metrics**
> Metrics help us understand whether or not we're improving and how we can further improve. Without metrics we can't improve!

That's how marketing works these days – by giving people a consistent feeling that you're *their type* of firm, that they already know you, and that they can trust your advice to be consistent and right for their business. Always keep in mind that you're building trust. At the highest, purest level, you're building relationships with prospects and buyers before they ever become a client.

At least 70% of your prospect's work is done before they actually meet you

Every single piece of content scales your ability to build a relationship through trust. Every video you create saves you having to repeat that concept or answer ten times, fifty times, a hundred times. It encourages your prospect that this is not the first time you've handled their question – even before they knew to ask it.

Remember too that as an accountant you're working from a point of distrust: they may have been let down by their accountant, or they may not know what an amazing accountant is actually like. You may have a way to go before they realise how great a relationship with your firm can be for their business. Think of your ROO metrics as a bridge between developing relationships with potential clients, and seeing more leads come into your firm as a result. Every social post, every article, everything you do builds that trust a little more.

Not everyone will approach you at the same pace. Not everybody will check you out when they need a new accountant. There are some people who think their accountant is perfectly fine, but they don't know what it's like having an accountant who makes their life and business easier – so they need to

> **Remember too that as an accountant you're working from a point of distrust**

be educated. You can help them realise that they can actually be motivated, and look forward to a meeting with their accountant. That the call from their accountant is one they would never ignore. That the day going through the business accounts is the best of their month.

> **You need to make an opportunity for people to understand how awesome you are, but don't expect the process to be immediate**

With all this long-term trust building, you may be wondering what happens to the measurement. Do you measure anything? Or do you simply share knowledge and build trust and hope it all comes together? It's still critical to measure how you're doing in marketing. You tell your clients that 'what you can measure you can manage' – and the same is true for marketing. Absolutely measure your marketing metrics, the key is to measure all of them. As many as possible. Every number, every platform, every format. Then you can look for patterns.

> Daniel Priestley's book *'Oversubscribed'* talks about how his company tracks everything. Every number available to them is tracked and recorded. However, when they're doing a particular campaign they only do the analytics once the campaign's over. To begin analysis during the campaign would dilute the team's energies and focus, but afterwards they can review what happened, what patterns are emerging, and how that knowledge can be used to improve their next campaign.

Think back to ROO. What is your objective? What matters to you, and what matters to them? Measure every single number that could possibly direct you to seeing changes relating to these objectives.

As accountants, it's really tempting to think your goal is to get more leads, and ultimately more clients. That is, of course, the highest goal, but you can't get there without first raising awareness, which is why a step-by-step process is so important.

Unlike the traditional view of what a lead is, you can see that your marketing leads are anyone you're building a level of trust with – even if they haven't enquired about your services yet.

Karen Reyburn summarises the Content Marketing Academy's Chris Marr's stages of raising awareness

1. **Is anyone actually consuming your content?**
   As you get into a consistent frequency and level of publishing, it can feel as if you're tossing your precious work into a big black hole. Check the data. What are the page views? What's the traffic? How many listen to your podcasts? Measurements that reflect whether or not people care about our content are the first phase of ROO metrics.

2. **Is your content creating conversations?**
   You're building relationships, so you're not looking for leads straight away. Look at likes, shares, comments, replies. Review the emails and messages you receive. Are you making an impact on peoples' lives, or are you simply talking? Measure what helps you notice the level of conversations you're having with prospects.

3. **Are you generating leads through content?**
   Now we get to the point all accountants are desperate to answer… or is it? What is a lead? Is it someone who says 'I want a quote for your services', or is it someone who downloads resources and signs up for your emails? This reflects whether the trust is building up to the point where people are getting a little closer to us. Are they asking for information, or enquiring about things? Measure what will help you tell the difference between the types of leads you're getting.

4. **Are these leads converting into sales?**
   Finally. Actual new business, new clients. You've converted a stranger or a sceptic into someone who wants to discuss their business with you.

Turning strangers into visitors

People are willing to spend between 15 and 40 hours of their time researching – not just one potential firm, but many – before they get in touch. They'll read articles, view your website, check you out on social media, watch videos. They are engaging with you to make sure their decision is a good one.

This isn't merely true about new prospects who never heard of you before. As many as 48% of people who have been referred to you already – been told you are excellent and good value and it's worth contacting you - may never ultimately engage with you because of the quality (or lack thereof) of your content. They may dismiss your firm – even though they've been referred – because your brand is outdated, your website doesn't work on mobile, or there's no way to get in touch using their preferred means of communication.

At the highest level, you need to attract people who are searching for particular information. Answers to their questions, solutions to their problems. You know what these issues are because they're common to your existing clients, and you've shared helpful information to those who are looking for it. You can pay a lot of money to have your website pushed to the top of the search engines, or you can simply create content that will do it organically and naturally for you.

To do this, brainstorm and jot down ideas whenever they arrive. In every meeting with clients, emails you send, discussions with the team, write down the questions they ask. The problems they face. The issues they need solved. Make notes about the type of client you don't want as well as the type that you do. Make notes about what you can share that will show who your firm truly is, and the individuals within it. Share content reflecting your values, your specialities, what you stand for, how you do business.

Developing your sales progression model

Not everyone is ready to buy today. Don't expect people to jump from nothing (no awareness of your firm at all) to signing up for a high ticket level of service on a monthly basis. Most people won't. Instead, build a progression model that will gently lead the buyer through growing levels of trust and confidence. And let them come when they're ready, with no pressure.

Awareness

Until your prospect knows you exist you can't help them at all. To rise up the ladder of search engines and get high enough for Google to identify you, you need to produce blogs, social media and guest content. For some, this development of awareness takes years, while for others it's months. But the more content you already have, the faster this process is likely to be. Once you feature in Google searches you need to maintain it too, so consistency is vital.

Free resources

This can be downloads, events, checklists, guides....anything that tells them how to solve their problem. You won't solve the problem for them – they need you for that – but they'll realise you know exactly what you're doing related to their pain points. Anything you can produce to help leads see who you are and how you want to help solve their problems will go a long way to encouraging them to move to the next step.

Small paid things

Small products and services at a low ticket value are what most accountants are missing. If you're asking a prospect to move from things that are completely free to paying several hundred or several thousand a month with your firm, you may need something in between those numbers. Consider offering a paid session or workshop. It eases the transition from stranger to client, and will help them test the waters by showing a little commitment on their part, without going all the way in yet.

Longer term paid things

You don't want any random leads. You want highly qualified leads – people who really get what it's like to have a relationship with their accountant and are willing to pay for it. If they've moved through the previous stages, it won't be a big step from the previous one to this. Most accountants expect prospects to leap from stage 1 to stage 4 instantly. Building in stages 2 and 3 helps ease the process along.

Big projects

Now that you've built an amazing client relationship, they will come to you with any problem in their business or life. Sales, mergers, acquisitions, disputes, planning… no matter what they face, you'll be the trusted accountant they come to because you've built trust over a series of stages.

Keep it simple

Building a full marketing plan with SWOT analysis and demographical research may feel productive (and will likely be very expensive), but the ever-changing marketing landscape means that by the time you put all that together, it will have changed anyway. Skip the complex marketing plan that no one understands or uses anyway, and move to simplicity. Know who you're creating your marketing for, what their issues and problems are, what you have to offer them in your progression model. Create specific marketing actions for every stage of your progression model. Track everything that reflects back on this progression model. Test, try, measure and repeat.

Test, try, measure and repeat

You can still talk about opportunities available to your firm, and risks facing you. But your marketing plan doesn't need to impress anyone. Better to spend all that writing effort into blogs, content and other things your clients might read or watch. (And if you can't get to the point in a few minutes, you probably don't know what the issue is.)

Your marketing plan can be as simple as a shareable spreadsheet with lots of campaign to-dos. That's what we use for ourselves and our clients, and we recommend you use it too.

When creating your marketing plan

- **Know your audience**
  If you don't know who all this marketing is for, you won't reach them. It will be vague and generic, and in trying to appeal to everybody will end up impressing nobody. Many accountancy firms say that their audience is something like 'privately owned SMEs and business owners making £500,000 to £500 million in sales'. That's not specific enough. Drill down. What industry? What types of people? What do they stand for? What kind of business do they have? Your buyer wants you to be incredibly specific – because they don't have time to filter all the accountants until they find the perfect one. Impress them instantly by creating content that will make them say, 'This is me! This is exactly my issue! They get me.'

- **Create a detailed list of what you are doing, and when you're doing it.**
  We'll start blogging next month' is too vague. 'We're producing three blog posts per week, written by this person, that person, and myself' is more like it. Make every action on your marketing list one that can be ticked off as achieved, on its own (not so broad that it requires multiple actions to achieve it).

- **Always include a call to action.**
  Your buyer is taking in a vast amount of information and knowledge on a constant basis. It's very likely they won't even read everything you put out – they'll skim. They still want to decide what they will do, but make it easy on them by suggesting the one action you suggest they take in every piece of content. Be very specific and don't give confusing messages. Many accountancy firm websites have up to 16 calls of action on the home page alone (phone number, email, arrange a free consultation, download this book, download that guide, click here, click there…it's extremely confusing and may cause your potential buyer to give up and go somewhere else).

- **Include both long and short term in your plans.**
  Have a foundational level of content that continues faithfully and consistently, day after day, month after month. Regular blog posts and articles, custom content creation, videos, website pages, social media posts. You can switch focus to different niches and audiences at times, but keep this foundational content going and don't give up. At the same time, you will also want to look at short-term campaign plans from time to time, to deliver additional marketing actions related to one specific item. This could be telling your clients about the latest app or technology, or inviting them to an event. Remember that your campaigns and your foundational content have to go hand in hand: neither of them can stand alone and deliver the results you want.

And finally

'Content marketing brings together the very best of you and your firm. It takes your expertise to the right buyers, prepares them to buy from you, and helps ensure that they are buying at the right time.

'It's a longer game than some of the short term solutions you may be tempted to try, but it's a better one by far. You're building a future for your firm, and a profitable one.' **Karen Reyburn**

Chapter 9

From APIs to Xero and beyond

. . . .

There's a whole load of stuff going on in the industry, with changing client expectations and digital tax requirements forcing people to do things in ways they wouldn't ordinarily want to. A lot of changes and opportunities support the concept I refer to as 'the digital practice', and are about digital transformation and recognising technology as an enabler.

Change has been rapid, and is accelerating still. So it's becoming increasingly important to consider how to thrive in the digital age and how to evolve our business to maintain pace and stay competitive. You're reading this book, so we can assume you're interested in the fully digital practice, or at least in moving more of your firm to the cloud, so this chapter examines the steps you might take.

What can we gain from the cloud?

- Improved efficiency, enabling the automation of repetitive tasks and reduction of errors.
- Real-time data sharing, increasing accessibility and improving decision-making.
- Streamlined systems and processes.
- More automated processes, making your business more scalable.
- Compliance becomes a repeatable, easily manageable process.
- With the right data-management app, changes in MTD compliance requirements become technical problems that are the responsibility of your provider to sort, and apart from checking that they have fulfilled future requirements in a satisfactory manner, you can concentrate on business development.

But there's more

Switched-on clients – and make no mistake, millennials, who are more engaged in new technology and accustomed to shopping around for the service that best suits their business models – will catch out the unprepared firm. They will see what technology is doing, and ask: why, since the technology is now doing what you used to charge them for, you are charging the same; and why, since various apps exist to make their work and yours easier, you're not using them.

Going forward

So you decide to put your entire workflow in the cloud (or at least a good portion of it), but how do you decide on the workflow, and the tools that suit it? What are the constraints and how do we ensure we deliver efficiencies? Let's split that into three parts: what you can gain (which will help you prioritise); the way you manage your end-to-end process; and how to choose apps.

The same challenges, true for everyone, are biggest for firms that have built a compliance-only practice as they have more to change – and potentially more to lose. That's because the shift to advisory is what will replace the income that will be lost through the inevitable downward pressure on compliance fees. Recognising that data entry and automation is something that will be automated is a big part of getting that new approach right.

Efficiencies

Think about the components in the end to end process. Map them out. Identify elements of duplication, that have no value and take those ones out. Then ask what can we do to increase the efficiency. That's effectively taking more steps from the process. The process design then becomes more about the automation. Often the wrong people were doing the wrong job because it wasn't sensible for them to do data entry, so it's important to then look at whether the right people are doing the right things in each stage.

What you can gain

Improved efficiency

Good cloud systems enable the automation of repetitive tasks, reduction of paperwork, a reduction (and eventual elimination) of the reliance on spreadsheets, and reduce the risk of manual error.

Increased accessibility

Sharing data in real time is a huge benefit for everyone – whether clients, colleagues or anyone who needs access. With the right supporting infrastructure it also provides the opportunity for accountants, business managers and staff to work remotely.

Improved decision-making

Cloud systems and the timely availability of real-time data means that we can anticipate our clients' needs, and provide strategic and timely advice. While non-cloud accountancy practices are forced to wait first for the delivery of the data and then for its processing, being on the cloud means we can provide real value and perspective to our clients, thereby increasing mutual confidence and deepening the relationship.

Streamlined systems

The paperless office, once a dream, is now a reality should you decide to embrace it. No more practices overrun by paper records, your office need no longer be defined by the smell of paper dust. Cloud storage can be quick, efficient and secure, and any necessary HMRC inspections are far less unwieldy as a result.

A more conducive environment for great client service

Technology works in two ways: it creates new challenges and makes new offerings possible. Take a client doing bookkeeping in a very traditional way – they don't enjoy it and don't want to do it, but getting an accountant can be too expensive. We can deliver that same stuff using technology. By delivering bookkeeping it helps us help the client to free up time so that they can focus on the important aspects of their business.

Matt Flanagan of Bluehub on app choices

The world I work in has around 650 add-ons, each of which could be used with Xero. This increases by about 300 apps a year, and accountants are getting app-overwhelmed accountants need to reduce the apps down to what their client base requires. Trick is to get the number of apps down to twelve. Then, if an accountant doesn't want to use an app, give it to a non-accountant. Let non-accountants do the tech stuff, minimise your apps and you're off.

Equally, we're able to focus on things that make easy automation possible, and that helps the client spend more time on what's important. At the same time we have better data because we've managed the process, so know our data quality is high enough to be able to manage that information and help the client with it. That's an important part of the logic people have to go through – you have to do the bookkeeping to get better quality data, and you can't start helping the client with other services until this comes to pass. Also you have to have regular conversations with the client to understand what keeps them awake at night. Once you have both good data and regular conversations, you can understand how to provide support with advisory services.

Taking the majority of the boring processes from people empowers them, as does easy access to the information they require. Plus of course the ability to recreate and manage each business process consistently and transparently throughout the entire firm means everyone knows where they are and what needs to be done.

This Chapter

Once you've decided on your customers and your product and service strategy, it's important to plan implementation, choosing the right apps to support your own internal processes and helping clients with apps that help theirs. This chapter covers this process, giving some of the solutions.

Managing the end-to-end process

In 10 short years Farnell Clarke has grown quickly and was one of the first firms to become a 100% cloud-based practice. We teamed up with KashFlow in 2008, becoming their biggest partner firm until 2014. In 2015 we decided that Xero was a better option for our client base at that time, and we migrated 600 clients from one platform to another.

When I first started, I didn't like what I was using. In 2007, I did the things I knew about. I liked IRIS because it was familiar, and I still believe it's the best option. It processed tax accounts, job management and kept everyone out of jail. We used it from day one. It managed the accounts and delivered all the things we needed it to do. Going on from that, the challenge is that IRIS is still a desktop product. We were responsible for backing it up, and like many people we weren't that good at it.

Now we've migrated to a hosted platform. Somebody else is taking care of backup and data security for the few desktop apps we have left. In an ideal world everything would be on the cloud, but at least by getting the software onto a hosted platform we have access to service-based data that can be reached, manipulated and used in a similar way to the other products we use.

IRIS is just one example. I believed there had to be a way to solve these problems, and kept looking. We started to look at how to access accounts on the internet. We looked at early accounting packages. I didn't think they were good enough.

I had started using Twitter, and people there convinced me to look at a new product as they thought it did what I was looking for. That was KashFlow, which we implemented in 2008. This heralded a change in approach because it made me rethink how I'd run my business. Every one of our clients went onto KashFlow, and that enabled us to do things that other firms couldn't, giving us a massive advantage. It took a while – 12 months in all – to get to the point where we found the right apps, but by 2009 we were a 100% cloud practice and by 2015 we had become a truly digital firm.

When IRIS acquired KashFlow, the two platforms (KashFlow and Xero) were consistent, but between 2013 and 2015, it was more what Xero did – and what KashFlow did not – that made us decide to move our clients over. Good tech is essential to what we do, and we need to always make sure we're providing the best to our clients and getting the best internally too. We took on Receipt

Bank in 2012 and GoCardless soon after. We'll keep a watching brief on all the vendors on the market in case of future changes.

'Some of the late-adopting accountants are still using the cloud as if it was a pioneering word. Unfortunately it's not, even though there are a large number of firms who aren't yet using it. I get frustrated when competitors perennially talk about the cloud because I kind of feel it was five years ago. It's not a thing any more, it's just where we do business. The virtue is in using it with the right partner apps so you have seamless use of your data. You can ignore it for now, but HMRC are putting a marker in the ground with MTD and you're committing business suicide in the long term.' **Grant Smith**

Now, some years later, open APIs providing an ability to build customised systems are the norm. We built our own practice and client-management software on the basis that what we wanted didn't exist. It's an advantage – we can create an app that does the things we want it to do, and that facilitates our business into the future.

I think you have to look at the core products you're going to utilise to manage the end-to-end process in your digital firm. We structured our process into three groups: input, processing and output. This is a reflection of our compliance process, which goes through the three stages of bookkeeping, accounts and tax returns. 'Input' is about how we get data from our clients, 'processing' is what Xero does for us, then IRIS delivers final accounts and tax returns. That said, we also use Futurli for management reporting and Xero to an extent as well.

Input

How do you make it easy for clients to deliver the data you need as efficiently as possible? We felt Receipt Bank was the right product for us, so all our clients get the Receipt Bank app as part of our onboarding process. At this stage we make sure they can send in invoices, recording them in the app. Receipt Bank was an early innovator but there are other products that do this too.

Processing

I've always believed the right processing product is important to deliver the efficiencies we need. We wanted to use the right product to deliver the efficiencies early on, and the fact that we were early adopters meant we were more limited, but also that we had a little more influence for a while. We now use Xero and impose it on our clients as our system of choice.

Our view is that they're the market leader in development approach and functionality. They were first to really deliver effective bank feeds, which is central to an efficient cloud practice. Other players in the market now offer bank feeds. We still think Xero will continue to be first in the market on innovation around AI and machine learning. I think the key difference between Xero and the others was that Xero was born in the cloud, and so has a big advantage over others who migrated or evolved from desktop environments.

It's the understanding of and the power of the data that apps potentially hold that turns accounting on its head. I think they built a product with a view to disruption in the way accountants would provide services. They did well, and as a result of their disruptive tech, accountants have the ability to work very differently to the way they used to. But to do this they need to be aware of the changes, of the potential of the tech and of how the whole idea of a bank feed as opposed to ledgers becoming a prime data source changes accounting completely.

To repeat this, because it heralds a revolutionary approach, accountants have traditionally started with the sales and purchase ledger. However, Xero turned the idea on its head. Now bank feeds contain the core data. Whether or not people saw it, this means that Xero was disruptive in its nature from day one. Now Xero's focus is on the products around that, and they're about driving efficiency and helping accountants deliver the things they have to in the most efficient manner.

My view is that using a single platform is the way to go because it gives you maximum efficiency, but we've worked with clients who feel they need to offer multiple platforms to legacy clients and here is the perspective from someone who has a wider view.

CASE STUDY
Simon Edrich of AccountsCo on providing multiple platforms

We use Business Central by Microsoft. It's infinitely scalable, versatile and it integrates with the Microsoft Dynamics suite and all of the office 365 products (word Excel sharepoint etc).

We have a 4 tier offering. The lowest, which we do in the office, is called VT. It's an Excel based piece of software at £90 a year in 2018. It has limitations, particularly around foreign currency work and it isn't on the cloud. Next we use QuickBooks with price point £7.50 a month in 2018. It's on the cloud and is pretty good but also has limitations. Next is Xero with price point around £27 a month in 2018. It's a great bit of software and integrates with loads of stuff. The trouble is that clients have to buy a load of apps and that can get expensive really quickly. It's also like a jigsaw, and trying to get all the pieces together when they're all designed separately is difficult. Business Central is no more expensive than Xero, but it takes a lot of configuring, so the cost is in the configuration rather than the apps themselves.

We decided to provide a 4-tier offering because there is no one bit of software that does everything, especially because if you want to consolidate accounts from different branches you need your own interface or top end software like Business Central, SAP or Sun Systems.

SAP is an ERP (enterprise planning) system and does everything from stock control to workflow. It would be a massive overkill for many companies, but at a certain size it's useful. You could try to consolidate all the accounts on a spreadsheet, but that would mean you can't do the management accounts quickly, and spreadsheets get complicated quickly, especially if you are consolidating multiple currencies.

We used software to meet our clients needs and grew into Xero. It is a fantastic bit of software, but there is no guarantee that the functionality you want is in an app. You could very well find yourself going down a route and discovering there is nothing that works, while Business Central is configurable in itself. That's why we now use Xero as our core product and configure Business Central around that core.

It is expensive to put stuff on the cloud. A proper Dynamics implementation would take a year, and that means someone is working on your system all the time. That person isn't cheap and represents a £100,000 investment. Then once you get into it you're handcuffed. You can't ever loose that support, you are continually tweaking systems and processes and such things can only be done for the expert. so it's not for the faint hearted.

That said, we are happy with it. We have evolved a special set of processes and have automated to the level that we have excellent KPIs for internal and external work. The next step will be formalising our continuous improvement.

> **Nowadays our clients can take a photo of a receipt, chuck the receipt in the bin and forget about it**

Output

Output for us is the annual compliance, so for this we use IRIS which produces our statutory accounts and tax returns. We then Futrli for monthly management and dashboard reporting where Xero management reports don't cut it.

Other apps

Apps are increasingly important. The fact that we can do so much on our smartphones – essentially keeping the business moving irrespective of our location – has huge implications. Mobility, ease of reporting, transaction processing, business confirmation and more means loads for our clients.

Receipt Bank changed the game – even for us, when we started using it in 2012. Nowadays our clients can take a photo of a receipt, chuck the receipt in the bin and forget about it (although we advise clients to keep their receipts until after the end of the VAT quarter). No more sticking everything in an envelope and putting it in the post.

GoCardless

GoCardless is an online direct debit specialist that manages the entire collection process on a client's behalf. Merchants can either collect and manage their payments using a simple online tool or integrate with cloud accounting software to automate accounts receivable.

GoProposal

We are constantly looking for new technology that improves our process. You'll get an idea of the significance of the use of GoProposal in our practice from the onboarding chapter. It closes the opportunity for scope creep and enables transparent, repeatable processes so all our teams understand what others are doing. Since adopting GoProposal we have become more certain that we are managing both expectations and costs.

The cost of adoption is minimal, and we were using GoProposal within 24 hours of signing up. Yes, of course there's a bit of preparation to do, but it come preloaded with data and you can look at it and – as we did – start sending out proposals within 24 hours. Once you start using it, you begin to identify other things you can do, which means business and internal operations can change quickly and significantly as a result. It has also had a huge influence on our cash flow and getting paid on time.

Whilst we use GoProposal for its pricing element we talk to a lot of firms that rave about Practice Ignitition as a tool for automating the onboarding process.

Practice Ignition

Practice Ignition provides accountants with a hybrid product, a smart proposal & payment solution built by accountants, for accountants. Firms using Practice Ignition have been able to eliminate their debtors and increase their monthly recurring revenue by over 40%.

▬▬▬▬▬

CASE STUDY
Farnell Clarke

Apps Farnell Clarke uses and likes:

- Chaser
- Deputy
- GoCardless
- Receipt Bank
- Workflowmax

- COG HR
- Flowdock
- IRIS
- Stripe
- Xero

- Datamolino
- FUTRLI
- Ocrex
- Tripcatcher
- Xero work papers

▬▬▬▬▬

And finally

I make a point of understanding the marketplace because helping clients automate their business is a big part of our service. We also need to stay ahead of the game ourselves to maintain the interest of our chosen sector. Our client base – new millennial businesses who are excited by new tech and are happy to take small tech risks to gain more efficiency – are happy with this approach, and so am I. Helping clients automate their business is a big part of how we are building our growing firm.

It's really important. The biggest thing that's happened to the market over the years has been the impact of new tech. The advent of the smartphone has had the biggest impact on the way we do business – not just because phones are powerful computers but also because of the development of apps that make our lives easier. What I can do today on my smartphone and what that means for our clients is just the start, so as we develop our fully digital practice, I always have an eye on creating structures that can be easily updated in the future.

The more automated your processes are, the more scalable your business, and once your data is on the cloud, updates and compliance reporting becomes a repeatable, profitable act. No more worrying about whether you have the capability to take on more clients. No more worrying about whether or not you'll manage after the implementation of MTD. You do your bit and the rest is up to the software vendors. That last point is another reason why you need to be able to keep up with new developments and know how to select best of breed.

Chapter 10

The onboarding process

· ·

T he importance of a seamless, repeatable onboarding process can't be overestimated. From the client side, it is an in-depth introduction to the firm's culture and a way of determining the trustworthiness, professionalism and competence of their selected firm. From the supply side, it is an opportunity to set up honest communication and trust, and to begin to understand clients' underlying requirements at a level that will help us suggest value added services in the future.

A positive first impression followed by a good, friendly professional level of communication is the foundation of the kind of relationship that our clients will want to share. More than this, though, a repeatable onboarding process is a way to obtain data in a consistent, ordered and timely manner. This will prevent stressful last-minute requests for information close to filing dates and a way to ensure uniform and transparent pricing structures throughout the firm.

Why a consistent, uniform and transparent onboarding process is important

- Ensures consistent data of known quality in advance of reporting periods, thereby preventing last-minute requests for information close to filing dates.
- Enables us to dictate our process to any new client.
- Ensures seamless handover to account management.
- Means that referring clients have demonstrably similar experiences.
- Ensures that clients' expectations are managed from the start.
- Enables transparency of process and related fee structure.

But there is more

Just being up front with people is important. Transparent, repeatable onboarding processes make it clear that our process is effective, will work and will benefit our client and that any other migration will not produce efficiencies. This is how our fixed-price structure works, and by sharing it with you I hope that you'll be able to take what is appropriate for your firm and avoid some of the worst inefficiencies from our experience.

This Chapter

We'll examine the bigger picture, including how the fully digital practice works in detail throughout this book, because both context and details are important. That's why this chapter goes into detail about the onboarding process – what we have found to work and how we've approached various efficiencies and challenges along the way.

The Workflow

Client engagement and Onboarding best practice

Thinking how a complex process that is regularly repeated might cause challenges and inefficiencies if it's not consistent and transparent makes a strong case for the transition to an entirely digital organisation. With this in mind, I'd like to introduce you to Rebecca, who will take you through our onboarding process at a fairly detailed level.

The onboarding process is not just about getting our new clients on board, collecting and collating their information. It is also a process of getting the right level of client engagement and training expectation management. We train the clients, and provided they follow our processes, our fees are right. If they don't then our fees are wrong, and we might have to have a conversation about increasing them, which has become more manageable through the way we use GoProposal.

Now they're stable, we're in the process of documenting and refining these processes. However, I expect that we will review them regularly in the future to make sure we're evolving best practice to enhance our client experience.

Client Acquisition

We evolved our onboarding process several times to arrive at what we have now, but it originally came about because we needed to establish a consistent and repeatable process. New clients sometimes got lost, or at least if they didn't we didn't ask for everything we needed from them in a timely and efficient manner. It wasn't just that we had diverse ways and timings for requesting vital information (such as clearance requesting) but also that if one person recommended us to his friend we wanted to make sure they both received the same experience.

The first formal part of the process sees me responding to the initial contact form, although this is often done by me when potential clients first contact us. This is usually by phone, partly because that's how our clients refer us but also because we have a high profile on Google which is very helpful. I then go back to the client to find out more about them. After this chat we'll send out a proposal for our fees from GoProposal (sometimes I'm able to do this during our conversation, so the client gets our proposal as soon as they put down the phone).

To start with I ask a number of basic questions that establish the pain points. Things like:

- why are you leaving your current accountant?
- what needs are not being met?
- what are your plans for the future?

This may sound like a question and answer conversation or formal interview, but it isn't. We want a more personal relationship and we start it here, with a personal approach. Some people aren't happy with this kind of approach and don't want it, at least at this early stage. They say things like 'I just want a monthly cost' and that's fine. One person wouldn't even give me an email address, but a lot are happy to talk because the price is not the only thing they are looking at. Where the only objective is price, they will not be the right client for us.

Establishing a starting point is slightly different with older, more established or traditional firms as the transition can be more painful. I talk to them about adopting software, try to get the message across that it's not going to be possible or cost effective for them to continue this way very soon because of the MTD VAT. A few have said they would rather deregister for VAT. That wasn't quite what I had in mind! It's up to them of course, and I'll follow up with another conversation in the future.

In some cases, you can tell if the client isn't going to accept. The fee might be too much, or they might be shopping around. Some are very price sensitive and aren't considering the services. Others might not have started trading. We have a follow-up process where we try to touch base with a client who hasn't accepted where we ask for their reasoning. Our findings for the follow-up process have been quite illuminating. Some who haven't responded haven't written us off, but are so busy in their day-to-day work that they've not had the time to answer. Sometimes we can help, once we know. This really extends and crosses over with our sales processes.

> Our findings for the follow-up process have been quite illuminating. Some who haven't responded haven't written us off, but are so busy in their day-to-day work that they've not had the time to answer

Often people mention that their accountant isn't using Xero and they aren't getting the support they need and thank us for contacting them. They ask us to come back in a couple of weeks.

Once we've got the information, we confirm with them that we've correctly understood them. Then we work on the proposal. Are they already on Xero? If not, we consider what work might be involved, what records they're currently using, how they're keeping stuff up to date. There is a lot to cover and in that first phone call. We don't want to flood them with everything so we don't necessarily cover it all at once.

Providing Client Options

An example of this would be if someone currently uses Sage Desktop. We have two options for them: start afresh on Xero or do a data migration for a one-off charge. We haven't gone into any detail yet, but we will warn them of the possibility of a charge because we need to set expectations. Sometimes I check their year ends with Companies House. If they have already paid for accounts with their current accountant I don't think it's fair for us to charge for that, so I might advise them to finish the year off with their current accountant before moving to us. Similar grey areas to this sometimes come up. However, if they say they don't want to use Xero that's the end of the conversation for us.

Flexibility of using GoProposal

You can send the actual estimate resulting from the conversation if they want it. The nice thing about GoProposal is that if they don't necessarily want an aspect of our service – or even the whole service – right now, we can indicate this with a star. Then GoProposal tells them what the prices are for what they want, and what they might be in the future. This puts it in the back of the mind should they decide that they want more.

Showing we've listened

At the bottom of our GoProposal document is a quote section. I like to note down some of the important things they've said about what they want from their accountant and where they see themselves in five years. If they say 'in five years I want to be lying on a beach' we can ask how we can support them in getting there, or if I feel I already have something that would work I can put that down too.

"It is often the little things that matter, and with the right choice of apps they can become a consistent part of our engagement. In this case by adding something personal, we are showing the client we're listening and the process helps both sides engage." **Will Farnell**

Some people need emails with specific answers to their questions. I tend to send a separate, additional follow-up email. Some people just click 'accept' quickly but that usually happens only if they have been referred. You wouldn't expect someone to sign up to anything for monthly payments without having thought things though, so most take a little more time. We get a few people who don't say anything, so we'll follow them up and ask if there's anything we can help with. Then the majority come back with more questions and it will take a couple of calls or emails for them to feel happy enough to sign up.

Getting the Onboarding Ball Rolling

We get the ball rolling immediately our clients have signed on. The administration process begins when we ask them for their current accountant details so we can send off a professional clearance letter. We always ask when we can do that. I would find it disrespectful if we received a clearance letter without warning, so I try to pay the courtesy that I would like to others.

We set up everything that is needed on our own internal systems. Our CRM documents everything, sets the jobs up, saves engagement letters and proposals, sends round an internal email to all departments to let them know we have a new client, how many directors there are, the payroll, what they do, the fees and then we send out the direct debit via GoCardless mandates.

> **We have come to recognise this behaviour as a red flag, so we are tough up front to avoid wasted time down the line**

Then it's time to set up the client's software. If they don't already have Xero we invite them in. If they do, we ask for a transfer. Then we arrange any training required. From the institution of the direct debit to setting up the software and training takes less than a week, so if they tell us they want to start after a certain period we hold fire. But if they don't want training for six weeks that's fine by us, too. In the meantime I make sure the software is set up properly, send out bank fee forms and if they have an existing Xero account we make sure everything is as it should be.

Sometimes they are missing loads of bank statements, so we need to get the bank run right. Brand new companies have a separate to-do list that often includes incorporation. We can't do Xero bank feeds until the bank account is open, so it can be harder for brand new companies unless they're properly on it.

It's surprising how many new clients sign up and then don't reply to us. We are learning to be quite tough about that. We have come to recognise the behaviour as a red flag, so we are straight with them upfront to avoid wasted time down the line. If they don't play ball, we let them know and they need to start responding or that's it. We looked at charging for a lot of the set-up but decided against it for now, which makes it important to get these things straight.

For us, we expect to include quite a bit in our basic charge. Other organisations aren't used to this, but it has always been our way. We have started to charge for training though. If the client does their own bookkeeping, the extra training takes at least two hours more. That's a sizeable chunk of our day and they need to understand what this represents in terms of opportunity cost as well as understand how to use the system properly.

Onboarding also includes registering them for different taxes, making sure that they have an HMRC account set up and getting them ready for MTD. We will try to book in our next steps – with them and in our diaries – so that we can turn everything around in a couple of months. We try to get them their years' worth of data and history turned around quickly and we're planning to reduce this further.

Exceptions

There are always exceptions. We had two weeks to service a client we took on last December. Another client was a nightmare because they were behind on their VAT returns. It was a chain of puzzles and we felt that we weren't getting the whole picture right up until the end of the process. The thing is, we are here to support them, and they know it, so we will keep reminding them, keep requesting the information. We're not afraid to ask if what we've asked of them is incomplete, and what has been ignored. Our clients appreciate it and know they need nagging. I often start my emails with 'I'm not nagging, but have you done this?'

> **It's not our way to say 'here it is and that's your lot', because every client is different**

I try to tailor training to the individual. If they are a brand-new setup and they have no data, a full set of Xero training is quite overwhelming, so I'll run through the basics with them. Then I'll have a call with them when the bank feed kicks in and from there I will decide what other training might be appropriate. It's important to give this sort of service and not just tell everyone to come and sit around a computer to go through a load of unfamiliar stuff they might not take in. It's not our way to say 'here it is, and that's your lot', because every client is different.

To make sure the training has sunk in and that we have the right data I will check the clearance information and make sure it agrees to the accounts files. I think it is good to highlight to the client that we're doing this. It's an effective way to make sure we won't start doing the accounts and only then discover we're missing stuff. Such lack of organisation would make us look like poor or inefficient accountants. We don't want to reach deadline day and discover we can't file because of missing basic information!

Onboarding often works more smoothly for people with manual records than with Sage desktop because the Sage software is often not compliant with the changes needed. Even so, we can demonstrate a much bigger gain in terms of efficiency once it's done, so our clients understand.

Part of my job is to contact those few annual fee payers still on our books and explain why moving to monthly payment is an advantage for all of us. Those still accustomed to a more traditional service need to be shown the benefits and that they will get more for their money. In a way this is no different to the way we onboard new clients and is an example where GoProposal comes in handy.

> ## Onboarding often works more smoothly for people with manual records

The Benefits of GoProposal

Before taking on GoProposal our client fees were a subjective thing. The person meeting the client would set them, in the main, and they might feel a little uncomfortable about whether the charge was correct because the benchmarks were kind of fuzzy. Now we can all charge the same, based on objective and tested criteria and feel confident in doing so.

Before GoProposal, you'd have a conversation over the phone with the client, then go away and think about it. Now I'll do the proposal as I'm talking to them. I can even send it over to them while we're still on the phone!

The GoProposal Process

When we first considered GoProposal we were looking at our fees anyway. I came up with a very manual system for the way we charged, and how to check we charged correctly. It's always a difficult balance and is regularly reviewed. Should we be charging for this, are we charging for that, and what is fair to include from both the client's and our perspectives? All questions we regularly revisit.

GoProposal comes with guidelines, but review of our charging structure must be an ongoing process. There will always be natural increases in costs, and as we become more familiar with how we are charging we will tweak the process.

When we set up GoProposal we started with limited companies and when we felt that was sufficiently stable expanded it to look at partnerships and sole traders. As part of the process we need to look at engagement letters, making sure the pricing structure is on them so that we have consistency in the future.

"GoProposal is a story in miniature, a demonstration of how efficiencies can be won using integrated tech on the cloud. Imagine how much more efficient a practice can be once everything like this is automated and you'll understand why I determined that Farnell Clarke should do this from the start." **Will Farnell**

Before GoProposal, the Onboarding was very individual. The service differed depending on who was undertaking it. I suppose we didn't have the opportunity to look at the big picture as a result. We'd just say immediately – "OK, if you'd like our service here's the bill!" Getting clearance information, making sure we had all the information, everything had been put into the software and all the steps had been followed in a timely way was idiosyncratic and sometimes got a bit lost. Now we have a separate Onboarding team and know that we can provide the same good level of service for every client, and have everything set up correctly and ready for service.

One warning I would give is this – when you think you have mastered the process realise that you need to add to it. For example, at the beginning we were thinking only of the company details and then realised we needed their tax information too. Once that process became stable we start a feedback process to see why they chose us and if we could do anything better from their perspective. With GoProposal we can be consistent and systematic, while at the same time accommodate different characters and their needs. After all, people are different and we want to serve them.

Efficiencies of a cloud based, fully transparent Onboarding system

- The entire team understand where each client is, what is required, what the state of the data is and how easy (or otherwise) it will be to file.

- The ROI of a uniform, consistently applied process is clear; fewer inefficiencies result from miscommunications, guessed pricing structures, last minute panics and more.

- With consistently applied pricing structures both client and firm can be confident of budgeting and their own internal ROIs.

- A clearly understood system is easier to tweak as new services, obligations and circumstances arise, with consequent gains in efficiency.

And Finally

A consistent onboarding process sets the stage for the future. We want our clients to trust us and to understand the way we work provides the best information and through efficiencies the best fee structure for them.

Only once have I taken on a client that I had 'that feeling' about, where, despite thinking I shouldn't take him on, I did. It was a nightmare. He was a process consultant so very protective in terms of his own processes. We tried to make his process fit with ours, but it didn't work out. We've learned from our experience and I hope that, by sharing this mistake and the details in this chapter that you can benefit too.

Chapter 11

De-Willing: letting go so your firm can grow

· ·

T his final chapter is a little different to the others. It discusses my experience of knowing when to leave your teams to it, when to stay engaged and how to lead without losing. I don't know whether Frances or James first came up with the word, but de-Willing is their shorthand for the way I am taking a step back from day-to-day operations in order to concentrate on strategy, business development and business alliances. Of course from my perspective, letting go of operational aspects of the firm is a little different, but the humour doesn't hurt and the title makes an important point. Ultimately you have a choice: build a valuable resilient firm, or stay the undisputed boss of something that will always be smaller.

It's all about growth

De-Willing is all about growth. The first thing with growth is I think it's actually really easy for firms to grow if they get the strategy and application right. Accountants know about many of the pitfalls. Of course we know it's easy to run out of cash, overtrade or make any of the numerous other mistakes all accountants know about.

Farnell Clarke has managed those anticipated pitfalls and grown fairly successfully for a long time, but fell into other traps instead. Because our expectations were unrealistic – we expected our year on year growth to slow down and stop – we fell into the early trap of making short-term decisions.

This has an impact. When you have 50 clients, having them all call you on a Sunday is not much of a problem. It's a different story with 500. As the numbers grow and you're no longer able to respond to client emails within five minutes, they call the office to find out if you are OK. I was advised that I should start setting expectations before getting to this point – and I'm passing that advice on to you.

> **When you have 50 clients, having them all call you on a Sunday is not much of a problem. It's a different story with 500**

Understand that if you set yourself up right and successfully deliver growth, there's no reason you'll need to turn business down – but you should be making long-term decisions from the start. We didn't think about how we'd scale because we didn't think we'd scale so steadily. That's why we failed to put systems and processes in place to support the firm as we grew.

The growth puts stress on a number of different areas, and as a result we only instituted regular staff performance appraisals after six years. That was late – with 20 staff it was already difficult to manage performance, and we hadn't set up anything to identify and manage when performance dropped below a level we were happy with. In the same few years we moved offices four times because we kept outgrowing what we had. There are lots more practical things that are easy to get wrong by

> **You should be making long-term decisions from the start**

not anticipating success. It's some years later now, and I see that period when we hit a wall as the time we recognised we needed to become more corporate in our organisation and business.

And that's the thing. Accountants have to recognise they are a business and can no longer continue assuming that they are different because they're a professional partnership. We have to consider growth and profitability – all the things that apply to our clients. How do we market? How do we engage? How do we develop the right products and innovate? Get that right, and plan for growth and then you can grow your business.

That's when you get to the point where the business owner can stifle his own business's growth. You can't be everywhere and can't be everything to every client. When I had 200 clients, I still knew every one of them. I wasn't the best at taking notes, and relied heavily on memory. A member of staff would say something and I would remember what I did two years before. Then I got to a point where I no longer knew everything that was happening, and couldn't be there for every discussion.

As the firm grows you also lose influence over the organisation's approach, values and the behaviours that brought you the clients in the first place. At that point you have to start relying on your staff to do things. Most business owners are control freaks, and it's difficult to learn to step away and leave *something* for someone else to do. You start with the mindset that nobody is ever going to do things as well as you do, but, as I think Richard Branson said, 'It's all about finding and hiring people smarter than you'. I've discovered that it's true.

Hang on to the belief that only you can do things properly and you'll never grow your business. Bring people on to take control for you. It's likely you'll get it wrong at times. You might hire the wrong people. You might hire the right people at the wrong stage of their careers. You might hire people with fantastic potential who aren't quite ready for what you want them to do. But you'll find ways of working through it and helping each person develop their potential or understand that they don't really want to be accountants.

> **Hang on to the belief that only you can do things properly and you'll never grow your business**

The other part of this equation is you need to get the client to accept that someone else will be their port of call. I had some coaching for this, and I adopted the habit of taking members of staff into meetings, introducing them by name and explaining they're in the meeting because they're far better than me and that they will also be faster to respond. This passing of the baton is an essential part of the process.

When James came in as MD, there was probably an expectation I'd be less good at letting go than I was. I think it was easier because we'd already got to the point where I'd accepted that what James would be doing wasn't part of my skill set. In fact it was a bit of a cop-out – he took a lot of the stuff I wasn't overly comfortable doing, like chasing bills and sorting out staff problems. That said, it was – and occasionally still is – harder to let go of some clients. I'd signed them up and worked with them for years, and we'd built up friendship, loyalty and respect.

> **I adopted the habit of taking members of staff into meetings, introducing them by name and explaining they're in the meeting because they're far better than me**

Handing over the management of your firm is therefore about recognising your strengths and weaknesses and building a team around you that covers all the necessary skills and Belbin team roles.

Now I'm back to doing the stuff I found exciting at the beginning. We were doing something different, trying to be really innovative and looking at better ways of doing things. As the business grew, I got more and more absorbed in operational management. Well, I wouldn't have had the time to write this book even two years ago.

The Belbin Team Roles

Dr Meredith Belbin, an expert in team work, observed that people in teams tend to assume different roles. He defined a team role as a tendency to behave, contribute and interrelate with others in a particular way and named nine such roles that underlie team success.

As the business owner I need to provide strategic leadership and work on the business, not in it. When you're absorbed in the day-to-day business you don't have the opportunity to step back and ask yourself why things aren't working as you expected or how they might be done better.

I now have time to have conversations about big ideas, build relationships with suppliers (which was what gave us our competitive advantage in our first five years), look at what the market's doing and look outside of accountancy to bring in models that improve the way we work. Now I'm back where I should be I can look again at how we do business and how we're going to stay ahead of the curve for the next five years.

Innovation is our strategy. Businesses that innovate and are first to market will, in most cases, do better than those who follow. We need to spend time remembering this to remain relevant and competitive in a very crowded marketplace.

I think it's fair to say the challenge for a majority of firms is that they're run the way we were running our business before James joined and took the operational aspects of the business from me. As directors, Frances and I were hugely absorbed in day-to-day client-facing activity. It leads to a lack of corporate approach and lack of commercialism – it's too big a job to step back and be strategic while running a client portfolio.

> **As the business owner I need to provide strategic leadership and work on the business, not in it**

James Kay on de-Willing

The de-Willing process has to be gradual and natural. Farnell Clarke had changed a lot as it grew, but because to all intents and purposes it was initially a family business, to go in hard with changes when I joined would have lost a lot of clients and staff. We didn't want to upset the apple cart – you can't change these things overnight. Clients and staff all know Will, and the organisational change that was part of the de-Willing process was not supposed to be a quick fix.

The de-Willing process evolved. We didn't plan to de-Will in any particular way, but for me it was about tackling the issues that Will and Frances hadn't had time for at all. The first part was me taking on those tasks and making clients aware that Will wasn't necessarily involved in the process. Then I took on fees, complaints and queries. Will was very good at forwarding things to me where clients had queries. Communication, both internal and external, were key.

> **We make sure clients push up the chain until they get to the right people and we educate them as to why and how it works better this way**

It was about getting a new structure in place and reinforcing that with the clients. They should go to their client manager – not Will. If there's a problem and they want to escalate it further, they should come to me – not Will. It goes in two directions. We make sure clients push up the chain until they get to the right people and we educate them as to why and how it works better this way.

Sometimes I think he finds it all a bit of a chore – especially when he's known clients for a long time. He can't know everything now though – the firm's too large for that. The structure is what it is and has to flow consistently. So, at the end of the day, having Will in the client communication process tends to cause issues or piss someone off. Keeping everyone on the same mission to achieve the same goal is more of a challenge than you might think. New clients come in and don't know Will, but the old clients take some education and it's not surprising Will feels loyalty to them.

We still have old clients and Will has a strong relationship with some. He forwarded me an email last week, asking me what we should be doing when a client had written that he only wanted to deal with Will on a matter. We're getting there. There will be quirks. Will likes a catch-up with people who are long-time friends or clients because of him, and that's fine – providing he brings in the client manager when he's had his chat, for consistency.

In the main, the first challenge for me was to understand the business and the staff. Some things couldn't wait. I was chasing outstanding fees within the first two weeks. Our first fee review went through within two months of my starting, and while Will had a strong influence in that, he's now not involved at all.

It goes hand in hand with the way we've changed the structure and team, and we're happy to charge more because we now know we have a good team doing a good job.

In the main, Will's left the day-to-day running of the business to me. Apart from when we have particular questions for which we need his knowledge, his only involvement is when I take decisions to the Board. I invite him to interviews for key staff and keep him posted, and Frances now deals with 90% of his old clients. He's got quite good at bringing in new clients, doing the proposal and letting the business do its thing, and when I ask his advice (often giving him a bit of background). The depth of knowledge he brings adds a reassuring weight.

Frances Kay on de-Willing

Sometimes Will gets enthusiastic about client communications and forgets the bigger picture. He still occasionally forgets to invite a manager to a client meeting or forgets to follow the process, which causes problems, because what has been said in the meeting doesn't necessarily get actioned or relayed.

I'm going through a similar process too and am looking forward to having the business de-Frances me. We have a new manager starting soon. I'm so excited because that will help me do my real job. Because of the staff shortage, I've been too directly involved with clients and not doing enough in business development recently, and feel I've done very little of my actual job while still trying to be part of the Board and participate in overall decisions. It's tiring to be picking up work that keeps you in the detail when you should be seeing the big picture.

> **It's tiring to be picking up work that keeps you in the detail when you should be seeing the big picture**

I can't actually be specific about how I'll be freed to work, but it will involve proper business development and the development of current clients. It would be nice to do a thorough review of our old clients, visiting them, and explaining the things we do they might have missed. Of course I'll take a manager or one of the team with me, so I don't get lumbered again! I also look forward to having the time to make sure the software's used properly and consistently throughout the company. Exciting times!

And finally

For me it's about getting others to share the load. It reflects a question I often used to get from clients, 'I have these really great employees – should I give them some shares?' When we think of the partnership model, it works quite differently. I got to a point where I couldn't sustain a business of our size with just one person taking ultimate accountability over everything else. I needed people with the same drive, motivation and ambition as me and that needed some ownership of the business. To an extent the buck still stops with me, but it was a real weight off my shoulders when I became able to share it. I feel lucky in that I recognised it was important to start bringing people in when I did, and am excited about the future.

Appendices

· ·

Acknowledgements

· ·

The thing with writing a book is it's an exciting idea. For me it's certainly an idea that has been bubbling away for some time but it's a daunting prospect! A few people suggested that all the stuff in my head should be written down. Thanks first, then, to Andrew Collings for pushing Xero to me for so long and persistently. Then thanks to the people who actually made it happen. Thanks to Iwona Tokc-Wilde for the all-important introduction to Carole Edrich who has made all of my ramblings logical and digestible, and without whom you would not be reading this! And to her team; designer Gavin Ives and editors Nicola Tann, Max Wooldridge, Jaime Breitnauer and Kamara Gray. We've also had contributions from some first-class thought leaders and industry pioneers, notably Karen Reyburn of The Profitable Firm, Paul Bulpitt of The WOW Company, Matt Flannagan of BlueHub, Grant Smith of Armstrong Watson, Simon Edrich of AccountsCo and Steve Cox from IRIS who contributed a wonderful foreword. You are all awesome. Thanks for your valuable input which widened the book's perspective.

I might have had the ideas, but delivery is made possible by a whole load of other committed people and the many partners we have worked with on the Farnell Clarke journey. My co-directors Frances and James have been fundamental in taking Farnell Clarke from an entrepreneurial firm to a scalable accounting firm. The roles they play allow me to do all the fun stuff over again; including writing this book, and working with some great firms, helping them go on a similar journey to the one we've played out for over a decade.

All of the Farnell Clarke team, past and present, have played their part in implementing the decisions – some great, some hare-brained – but it takes a certain kind of person to keep up with our rate of change. I take my hat off to each and every one of them. The same, of course, goes for our amazing clients, many of whom have been willing guinea pigs, trying out new tech as we go.

Then there are the guys who have provided the technology. KashFlow, Xero, IRIS and Receipt Bank have all played a hugely significant role in the development of Farnell Clarke. They've all helped provide the platform for me to write this book and work with other accounting firms.

Finally, none of this – not the firm, the book, or the consulting – would be possible without the support of my family. Thanks to my wife Jill, both my and Jill's parents for the consistent support they've offered, and of course to my children who have seen me heading out and sometimes disappearing for a few days at a time for many years.

So many people have been part of this journey – too many to mention individually – but to everyone that has engaged with me and Farnell Clarke and shaped our business and my thinking, thank you! I hope you enjoy this book, the end result – for now …

Will Farnell

'

Biographies

· ·

Will Farnell

Owner: Farnell Clarke Record shop owner and band manager through B2B sales is not the usual route to qualified accountant and business consultant but then Will is not your typical accountant.

Will is the founder of Farnell Clarke, an innovative and pioneering accounting firm based in Norwich and London, UK. He set up Farnell Clarke in 2007 having previously worked within a Big Four firm advising predominantly public sector bodies on efficiency and process improvement. From day one he had a desire for Farnell Clarke to be a different kind of accounting firm.

Under Will's leadership the firm's seen consistent growth averaging 36% year on year for the last 10 years. The firm has twice been named Best Independent Firm (East of England) at the British Accountancy Awards, and in 2016 was named Most Innovative Firm in the independent and overall categories.

Back in 2008, Will saw an opportunity to utilise technology to drive efficiency and change the way accounting services could be delivered to clients. Farnell Clarke was one of the first 100%-cloud practices in the UK and the way Will deployed technology in the firm was a significant catalyst in the firm's growth.

Will now uses the experiences acquired over the last 10 years as a tech-driven firm to support other firms in moving to a digital-based strategy. He's regarded as a thought leader on tech and the changing landscape and environment currently driving the accounting profession. Will is a regular speaker and advocate for some of the leading UK and global accounting tech brands.

Steve Cox

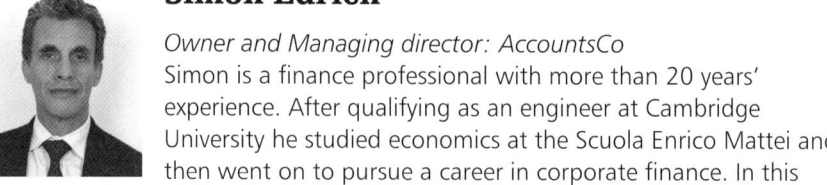

Chief evangelist: IRIS
Steve is chief evangelist of IRIS, a technologist and chartered accountant who looks at how technology can simplify the modern accounting world.

He joined IRIS in 2002, and has worked across most of the business since then, including customer support, engineering and product management. His most recent previous roles at IRIS include senior product director and interim CTO.

Steve has over 15 years' experience in technology and accounting, and works closely with customers, software companies, governing bodies and the government to champion the digital transformation of SMEs and accountancy firms in the UK

In Steve's current role as chief evangelist, he's looked across the globe at how technology and legislation is changing the role and requirements of the accountant and looking to the future to predict how the accountant's role will further evolve.

Simon Edrich

Owner and Managing director: AccountsCo
Simon is a finance professional with more than 20 years' experience. After qualifying as an engineer at Cambridge University he studied economics at the Scuola Enrico Mattei and then went on to pursue a career in corporate finance. In this role he worked on a number of high-profile transactions, including providing advice to the Italian Treasury on the privatisation and IPO of ENEL, and assisting the directors of Tatneft, a Russian state-owned oil company, on the company's privatisation, New York Stock Exchange listing and €300m Eurobond issue. In 2009 he left banking to set up AccountsCo, an accounting boutique that specialises in helping non-UK businesses set up in the UK. AccountsCo now boasts 10 professional full-time staff that service more than 300 clients. Simon has written numerous articles and spoken at various events and conferences. Simon loves work, business and all things Italian. In his spare time he enjoys sailing, windsurfing and spending time with his family.

Richard Hattersley

Practice correspondent: AccountingWEB
I am the practice correspondent on AccountingWEB, the award-winning online professional community with more than 100,000 members. I joined AccountingWEB in 2015 as a journalist before moving to my current position where I am responsible for managing and writing content for accountants in practice.

Rebecca Duale

Client services manager: Farnell Clarke
I joined Farnell Clarke three years ago from a traditional accountancy background. From the offset I loved Xero and personally took the initiative to speak to clients and explain the benefits of the software. This led to me looking at processes, training and the service level we provide to our clients, as well as working to improve client experience and profitability. By trade I'm a qualified accountant but my strengths are building relationships with clients and perfecting our services levels.

Paul Bulpitt

Co-founder: The Wow Company
Paul Bulpitt is the co-founder of The Wow Company and head of accounting at Xero. Paul founded The Wow Company in 2004, building a fast-growing national firm exclusively serving small businesses. Driven by a focus on personal relationships, a world-class client experience and simple processes, The Wow Company has earned numerous accolades and awards, including the Practice Growth and Practice Excellence awards. Paul's mission is to empower people to build beautiful businesses.

Matt Flanagan

Managing director: Bluehub
Matt Flanagan is a cloud business systems specialist, working in close partnership with forward-thinking accountants to support their transition to cloud accounting and developing relevant advisory services.
   He assists firms with their cloud journey to convert from desktop/manual ways of working to adopting and utilising cloud-based best practices.
   Matt engages with accounting firms in a number of ways with online workshops, online focus groups as well as physical think tanks and digital firm intensive groups.

Karen Reyburn

Managing director and owner: The Profitable Firm
Karen combines two skills rarely seen together: a qualification in accounting and an artistic mindset. A CPA in the US, Karen moved to Scotland in 2001, where she worked for and with accountancy firms, as well as running an international wedding photography business. In 2012, she set up The Profitable Firm, a creative agency that works exclusively with accountants.

Karen is a dual British-American citizen living and working in Scotland. Her creative agency is 100% virtual, with a core of 10 employees working from the UK, South Africa, Cyprus and the US to serve accountants all over the world. Karen speaks regularly for organisations such as Xero, the Institute of Chartered Accountants of England and Wales (ICAEW), BKR International, AccountingWEB and Accountex. She's fuelled by copious amounts of black coffee.

Grant Smith

Partner: Armstrong Watson
A partner in Armstrong Watson with over 25 years in the accounting industry, I've been partner for a number of years now, dealing with owner-managed businesses in all sectors. I have always believed in making businesses efficient and helping them grow through technology, so in 2010 when I was introduced to Xero I was sold and have since been an enthusiastic advocate. In 2012 we chose Xero as our firm wide partner of choice for accounting software, after which I continued to lead the move over to cloud accounting, and utilisation of all the benefits. In 2014 we achieved Platinum status with Xero, mainly because of the size of my client portfolio on Xero. Then in 2016 we changed our structure in to Service Lines where I joined the accounting service line leadership team and started converting over 3,000 clients to Xero. In 2017 we achieved Xero partner of the year.

Armstrong Watson is a mid-tier firm with 15 offices covering from Northern England up to the central belt of Scotland.

James Kay

Managing director: Farnell Clarke
Having dropped out of university after spending all my money, I decided on-the-job training was the way forward, and accountancy would be a good choice given I was quite good at maths.

I started studying CIMA at home and working in an accounts payable department of a builders' merchant in a team of about 100, matching invoices to orders for the Dudley branch. My career path from there was somewhat varied – financial services, oil and gas, manufacturing – but each move was a progression.

I finally ended up as financial controller for a charity fundraising call centre, where my career path changed. A management walkout over a weekend about two months after I joined left me sat on the main floor managing a team of 60 or so. The problem was I seemed quite good at it, the 60 grew to 200, and I was made operations director. In this environment you come across every situation possible – if it can happen, it probably will.

When it was time to move on I headed back to an accounts environment for a commercial property management company, but it was very much about people again, with a big team to manage and processes to maintain.

Then, in 2016, Frances and Will approached me with a new challenge. Having never worked in practice, I treat it like any other business. The staff are just people providing a service like so many other sectors. And despite what I was told about working with your partner, I'd find it pretty hard to not work with Frances now!

Frances Kay

Co-director: Farnell Clarke
Frances' career started in accountancy when her mother found a job advert in the local newspaper. After a mad dash into Norwich for a shopping spree and changing in the train station, she was ready for the interview.

She specialised in bookkeeping, VAT and management accounts and Sage desktop, and worked both in-house and onsite with clients. After cutting her teeth at a couple of firms, she accepted an offer from Will, one of her old ACCA tutors, in a growing firm of eight at the time. As a devout Sage lover the tech that Will was using was a little hard to believe but she quickly adjusted, and her role there quickly changed from business services to heading up a small team.

Becoming director was a challenge she tackled head on. The firm was growing quickly so there were new things being thrown at the directors all the time. The best part of her current role is reviewing and learning new software that can make a client's life easier. She loves regularly talking with clients so she can go further to help them – not just in their business, but everything else.

Glossary

· ·

A

AAT: Association of Accounting Technicians

AI: artificial intelligence

API: application programming interface

AutoEntry: automated data entry software

B

Blockchain: a software platform for digital assets

BlueHub: cloud software integration consultants

C

Companies House: the UK's registrar of companies and an executive agency and trading fund of Her Majesty's Government

CRM: customer relationship management

CSF: critical success factor

E

End-to-end process: all the work that needs to be done to achieve an objective or goal

Expensify: a software company that provides a travel and expense web and mobile application

F

FreeAgent: online accounting software

G

GoCardless: an online direct debit network that manages a client's recurring payments how and when they want

GoProposal: pricing and proposal software for accountancy firms

H

HMRC: UK Tax Authority

I

Intuit: accounting and tax preparation software for accountants, small businesses and individuals

IRIS: accountancy compliance software

K

KashFlow: online accounting software

M

Movemybooks: software that converts data from one accounting product to another

MTD: Making Tax Digital, the UK Governments initiative for digitalisation of tax

MYOB: an Australian accounting software company

Glossary

. . . .

O

Onboarding: the orientation process by which a new client or employee learns the ropes and culture of a new company

Out-of-house: work contracted out to an external company

Outprice: to sell at a lower price than another company/seller

P

Practice Ignition: client onboarding assistance software

Q

QuickBooks: an accounting software package

R

Receipt Bank: automated receipt processing software

RL: 'real life', as opposed to online or virtual

ROI: return on investment

ROO: return on objective

RTI: Real Time Information

S

Sage One: online accounting and payroll software

Sage 50: desktop accounting software

T

tech stack: all the tech and apps a company uses

W

webexpenses: an app to manage expenses

X

Xero: cloud-based accounting software for small- and medium-sized businesses